BEBBIS
for
BABIES

BEBBIS FOR BABIES

The Diet to Help You on Your Journey to Conception

By Dr. Robert Kiltz, MD

Printed in the United States of America

First Printing, 2024

ISBN-13: 978-1-962984-14-0 print edition
ISBN-13: 978-1-962984-15-7 e-book edition

Waterside Productions
2055 Oxford Ave
Cardiff, CA 92007
www.waterside.com

"Diet is the number one source of chronic inflammation. Making changes to what, when, and how frequently you eat can heal your body and reduce inflammation."

—Dr. Robert Kiltz

TABLE OF CONTENTS

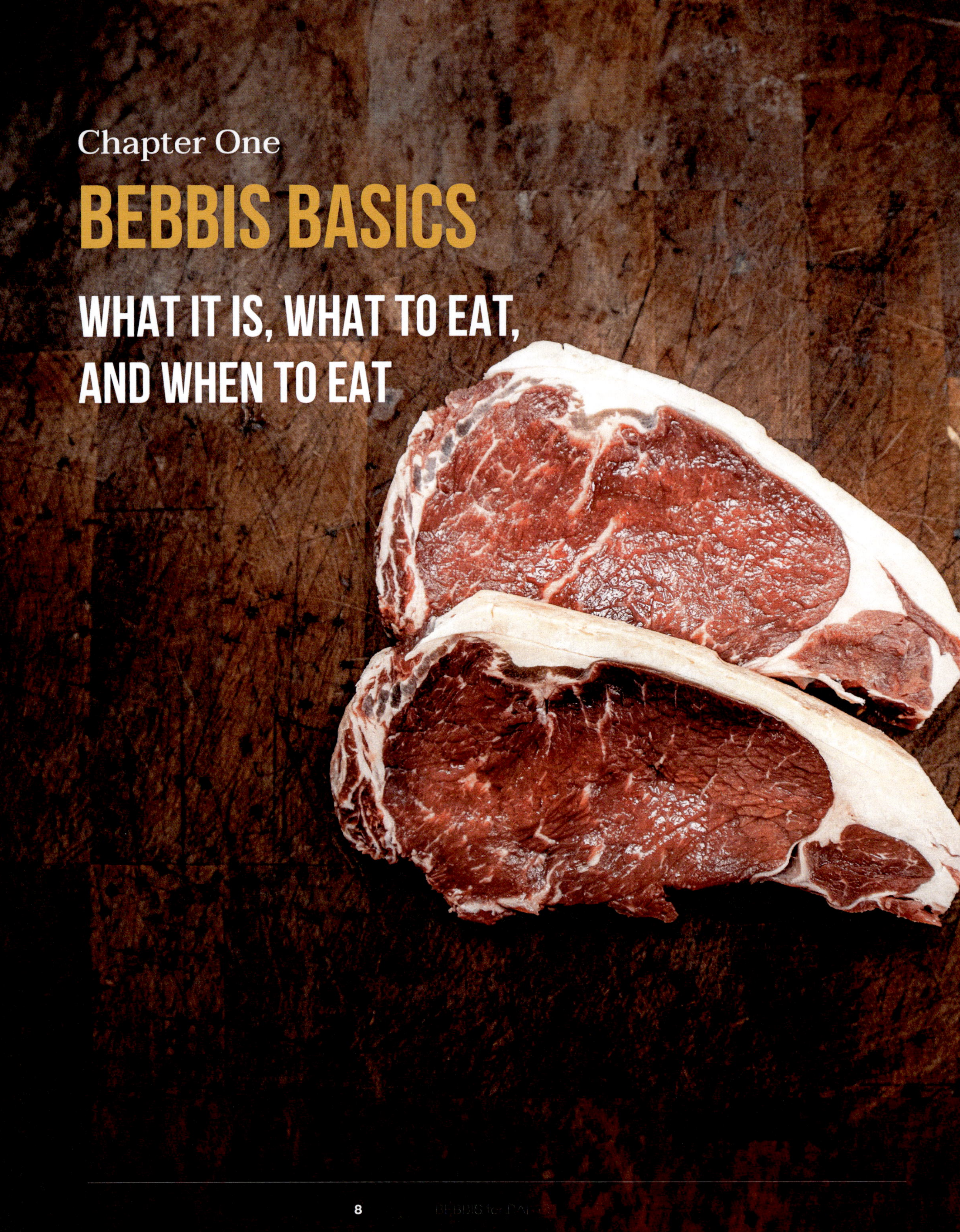

Chapter One

BEBBIS BASICS

WHAT IT IS, WHAT TO EAT, AND WHEN TO EAT

WHAT IS THE BEBBIS DIET?

Bacon

Eggs

Butter

Beef

Ice Cream

Intermittent Feasting

Salt

The BEBBIS (pronounced "babies") Diet is an approach to eating that focuses on consuming ideally one, but maybe two minimally processed, ultra high-fat, animal-based meals per day.

THE ACRONYM STANDS FOR BACON, EGGS, BUTTER, BEEF, ICE CREAM (KILTZ'S HOMEMADE KETO ICE CREAM), INTERMITTENT FEASTING (AKA FASTING), AND SALT, but the diet also allows for other fatty cuts of meat, including lamb, salmon, pork, bison, elk, chicken, etc. Along with other animal fats like lard, tallow and full-fat dairy like heavy cream and most cheeses.

Focusing your diet on these fatty animal-based whole foods dramatically reduces inflammation, protects you from the ravages of carbohydrates, eliminates exposure to plant toxins, and provides an abundance of macro and micronutrients for every cell in your body.

I developed the BEBBIS diet over a decade of experimentation and research in my clinical practice as a fertility doctor as a way to naturally improve fertility and treatment outcomes.

Through countless hours of research and the treatment of thousands of individuals with this diet, I discovered that not only did this high-fat carnivore-based diet dramatically improve both male and female fertility but that many of my patients were coming off other medications and drastically improving their lives in other ways.

Dr. Kiltz breaking fast and enjoying a plate of ribeye, bacon, and eggs.

WHAT TO EAT

Bacon

Eggs

Butter

Beef

Ice Cream

Intermittent Feasting

Salt

BEBBIS is a memorable rule of thumb for keeping you focused on the healthiest, most nutrient-dense foods on earth. Think of Bacon, Eggs, Butter, Beef, Ice Cream, and Salt each as a symbol of an entire category of nutrient-dense superfoods.

You don't have to only to eat these six foods, though you certainly can thrive on these foods alone and **many people will LOVE the simplicity of doing so.**

Fatty Meat

Ribeye steak, short ribs, chuck roast, brisket, NY Strip, 80/20 or fattier ground beef,

Lamb rib and should chops

Pork jowel or belly

Fatty fish and seafood like salmon belly and Atlantic mackerel

Skin on, fatty poultry duck or chicken wings

Nutrient-dense organ meats like duck liver and beef liver

Minimally processed high quality preserved meats - Prosciutto, Speck, Jamón Serrano and Jamón Ibérico, Coppa, Culatello, bresaolla, Pancetta

Eggs

Chicken

Duck

Goose

Quail

Ostrich

Even salmon or other fish eggs

Animal Fats

Butter

Ghee

Tallow

Lard

Chicken fat

Duck fat

Ice cream

High Fat Dairy

Heavy cream

Kiltz's Home Made Keto Ice Cream

Half and half

Most cheese (minimally processed high quality cheese is important)

Salt

Himalayan Pink Salt

Redmonds Real Salt

Maldon Sea Salt Flakes

Other high quality natural sea or colored salts

"Fat is fuel, so while all unprocessed animal meats are fair game, it's important to dip your meat in butter, particularly leaner meats like most cuts of chicken, fish, and seafood."

WHAT TO DRINK?

Still or Spring Water

Mineral Water

Sparkling Water

Black Coffee or Expresso

Bone Broth

Coffee w/ Butter or Heavy Cream

Plain Green or Black Tea

Tea with Heavy Cream or Butter

Unsweetened Naturally Flavored Sparkling Water

The first and best drink is spring, filtered, or mineral water.

Plain Tea and coffee or with a little bit of butter or a splash of heavy cream are also energizing and satiating beverages that fit in well with the BEBBIS plan.

Bone broth is a meal and beverage in one. In addition to providing hydration, bone broth delivers important electrolytes, collagen, and specific amino acids that can support a healthy body.

Alcohol is not a BEBBIS beverage–in fact, it's an inflammatory toxin, and if you're serious about your health, it's best avoided on all but special ocassions. If removing alcohol is too much of a challenge, try to cut it to at least once a week.

What Not to Eat

FOODS TO ELIMINATE

The BEBBIS plan eliminates all plant and plant-derived foods as well as processed foods and greatly reduces high-carb and ultra-lean animal products:

Eliminate

Greatly Reduce

When to Treat

"We are human, and that means we need a treat from time to time. My homemade, full-fat ice cream makes for a wonderful treat, but I understand sometimes you need something even "treatier." As long as you're eating BEBBIS-approved foods and having a treat like a cookie or cake doesn't completely throw you off the wagon, it's a-okay to have it from time to time. I personally have a non-BEBBIS-approved treat about once every 2-3 months when I'm celebrating with friends or family."

BENEFITS TO INTERMITTENT FEASTING

- Increases Human Growth Hormone Levels

- Induces beneficial cellular repair pathways

- Activates longevity genes

- Reduces and balances blood sugar and insulin levels

- Improved weight loss

- Reduces risk of type 2 diabetes

- Reduces oxidative stress and inflammation

- Improves heart health

- Improves blood triglyceride levels

- Improves blood pressure

- Reduces brain fog

- Lowers risk of stroke

- Increases levels of brain-derived neurotrophic factor

- Reduces risk of Alzheimer's

- Improves Gut health

WHEN TO EAT?

"Intermittent Feasting" commonly known as intermittent fasting means eating your BEBBIS meals during ideally one but possibly two meals a day. Ideally between 4-7 pm. This gives our digestive system time to process your meal, and then to rest and heal. Intermittent feasting also opens up time and mental space for focusing on creativity, relationships, and life goals.

Our digestive systems are designed to go without food for extended periods of time. For millions of years, it was probably rare for a human to eat every day. We would go days, weeks, and occasionally months without eating.

We're simply not made to process 3-6 meals a day with snacks in between. This modern habit fills our gut with fiber and carbs that ferment and feed overgrowths of bacteria and yeast in our gastrointestinal tract leading to leaky gut, chronic inflammation, infertility, and autoimmune disease.

I always recommend only one meal a day, but for some just starting their BEBBIS journey or those who are HIGHLY active, this may not be possible. Here are three intermittent feasting schedules you can try.

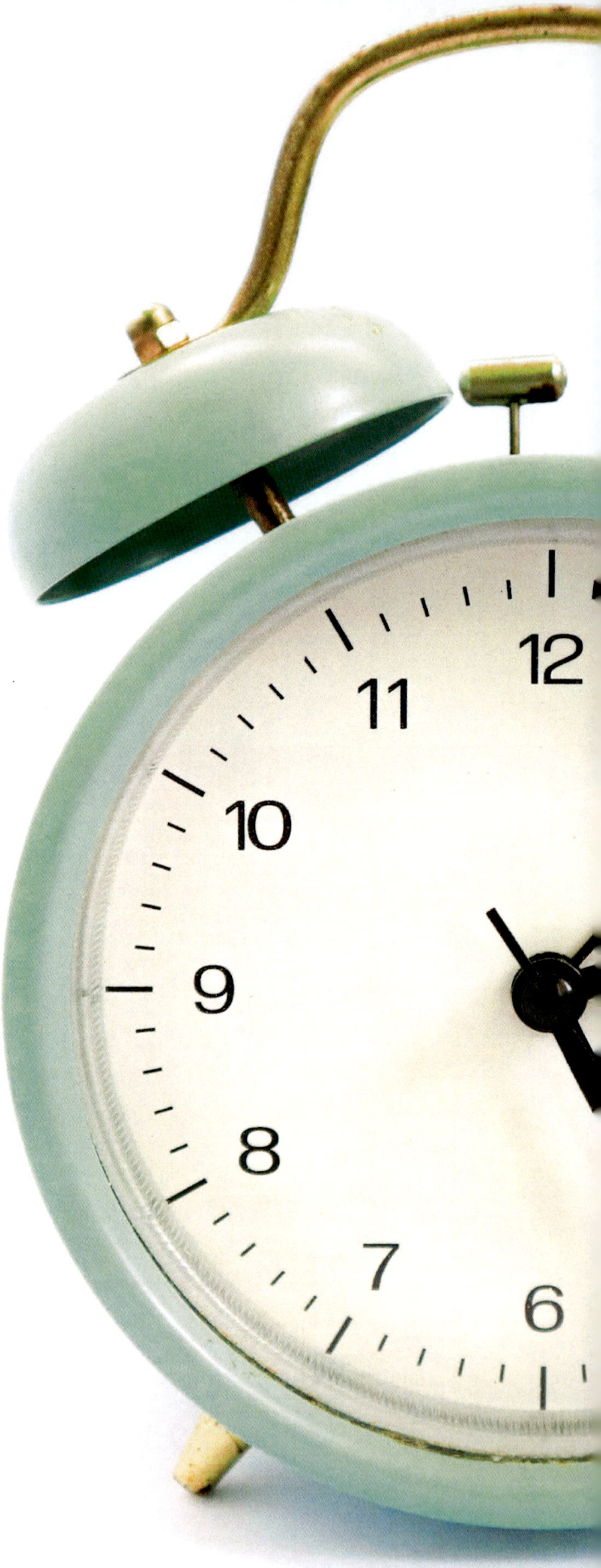

WHAT CAN YOU DRINK DURING A "FASTING" PERIOD

During feasting periods you can not consume anything with calories. That means no food or beverages like heavy cream or bone broth.

ONE MEAL A DAY (OMAD)

OMAD, or One Meal a Day, is true intermittent feasting and the eating pattern most humans should practice.

This method has the simplest rule but perhaps one of the most intense. **OMAD requires fasting for 23 hours.** The eating window is the same one hour period each day.

	DAY 1	DAY 2	DAY 3	DAY 4	DAY 5	DAY 6	DAY 7
Midnight	23- hour fast	23- hour fast	23- hour fast	23- hour fast	23- hour fast	23- hour fast	23- hour fast
12 PM	1- hour Feast	1- hour Feast	1- hour Feast	1- hour Feast	1- hour Feast	1- hour Feast	1- hour Feast
	Fast	Fast	Fast	Fast	Fast	Fast	Fast
Midnight							

THE 16:18

The 16:8 method is a great beginner schedule and introduction to intermittent feasting. If jumping straight into OMAD seems a bit overwhelming or ends up being too difficult when just starting out, I recommend falling back to this, getting comfortable with a daily 16 hour fast and then progressing back up to OMAD.

Fast for 16 hours a day consuming only water or plain coffee or tea during this time. Break your fast with a BEBBIS-approved snack, a glass of bone broth, or a meal; finish your last meal no later than 8 hours after your first food.

	DAY 1	DAY 2	DAY 3	DAY 4	DAY 5	DAY 6	DAY 7
Midnight	16- Hour Fast	16- Hour Fast	16- Hour Fast	16- Hour Fast	16- Hour Fast	16- Hour Fast	16- Hour Fast
12 PM	First Meal Around Noon	First Meal Around Noon	First Meal Around Noon	First Meal Around Noon	First Meal Around Noon	First Meal Around Noon	First Meal Around Noon
8 PM	Last Meal by 8pm	Last Meal by 8pm	Last Meal by 8pm	Last Meal by 8pm	Last Meal by 8pm	Last Meal by 8pm	Last Meal by 8pm
Midnight	16- Hour Fast	16- Hour Fast	16- Hour Fast	16- Hour Fast	16- Hour Fast	16- Hour Fast	16- Hour Fast

THE 20:4

20:4 is very close to the 16:8 method. The only differences are a longer fasting period and a shorter eating window. Fast for 20 hours. Eat during a four-hour window. Try eating between 4 pm and 8 pm (if your schedule allows) and fasting the other 20 hours of the day. This eating window can be broken down into two regular-sized meals, or one snack and one larger meal.

Your first bite of food could be a snack or an entire meal. If you're working your way up to OMAD, start with two full meals then shift to one snack and one meal.

	DAY 1	DAY 2	DAY 3	DAY 4	DAY 5	DAY 6	DAY 7
Midnight	20- hour fast	20- hour fast	20- hour fast	20- hour fast	20- hour fast	20- hour fast	20- hour fast
4 PM-8PM	Feasting	Feasting	Feasting	Feasting	Feasting	Feasting	Feasting
	Fast	Fast	Fast	Fast	Fast	Fast	Fast
Midnight							

HOW MUCH TO EAT

Now that you're eating more nutritious foods and less frequently, it's an obvious question - how much should you be eating each day? One of the easiest aspects of following the BEBBIS Diet is that there's no calorie tracking and you're not going hungry. You simply tune into your body and eat until you're full and satiated. No pre-historic man weighed his food, why should we?

Most meat-based eaters consume between 1-2 pounds of meat per day and find it unnecessary to measure portions. But it's important to ensure you're eating plenty of fat. On a meat-based diet, you can run the risk of eating so much protein that your body then converts it to glucose and uses it for fuel (this process is known as gluconeogenesis) instead of breaking down fatty acids into ketones.

Ensuring you're eating fatty cuts of meat will prevent your body from converting protein into sugar.

Dr. Kiltz recommends eating about a fistful of food a day (up to two fistfuls on occasion). A typical meal for Dr. Kiltz includes .... a dry-aged rib eye steak cooked black and blue under a broiler, dipped in melted butter, and sprinkled with Maldon Sea Salt. He usually eats one meal at night before bed. On weekends, he sometimes enjoys a breakfast of steak, bacon, and eggs to fuel his day. Dr. Kiltz doesn't measure grams or calories. He tries to keep a 1:1 ratio of fat to protein, 2:1 or 3:1 fat to protein is even better. Eat the fat, feel satiated, and you're done.

Your body has an amazing way of getting you to eat enough food to prevent any major calorie deficits or surpluses. But we get it. We've been conditioned to think we need to aim for a certain number of calories, **so here are a few sample days eating along with their calorie content and basic macro and micro nutrient contents.**

DAILY NUTRITIONAL EXAMPLE

Ribeye (4oz) and Simple Ground Beef Tallow

Morning

Food	Calories	Total Fat (g)	Protein (g)
Ribeye (4 oz)	330	25	27.3
Butter (4 tbsp)	204	23.04	.24
Total	534 cal	48.04g	27.54g

Afternoon

Food	Calories	Total Fat (g)	Protein (g)
Ground Beef (12oz)	853	67.2	57.69
Tallow (4tbsp)	460	52	0
Total	**1,313 cal**	**119.2g**	**57.69g**

Daily Nutritional Totals:
Calories: 1,847
Fat: 167.24g
Protein: 85.23g

You simply tune into your body and eat until you're full and satiated

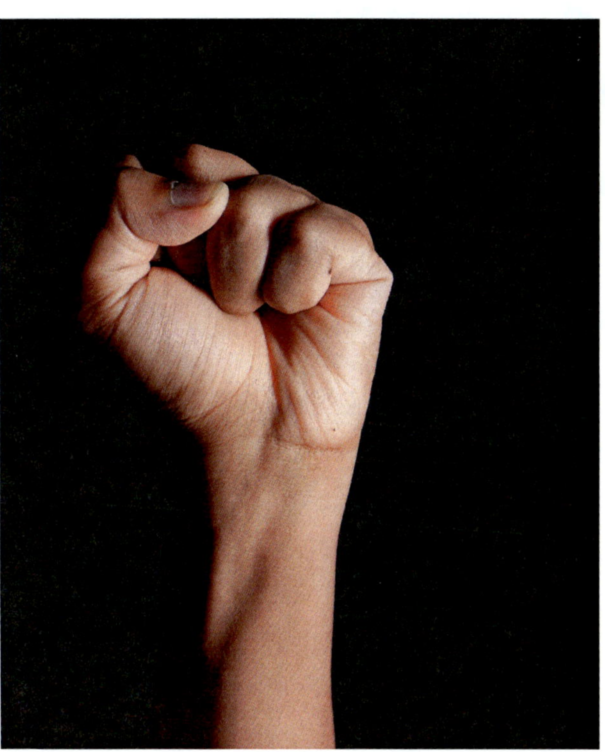

Dr. Kiltz recommends eating about fistful of food a day (up to two fistfuls on occasion.)

Chapter Two

SAMPLE MEAL PLANS

Month 1

DR. KILTZ PERSONAL 90-DAY MEAL PLAN

SUNDAY	MONDAY	TUESDAY	WEDNESDAY	THURSDAY	FRIDAY	SATURDAY
26	27	28	29	30	31	1 **5PM:** Ribeye Dipped in Blue Cheese Butter
2 **5PM:** Ribeye Dipped in Blue Cheese Butter **5:30PM:** 1 Large Scoop Kiltz's Ice Cream	3 **5PM:** Salami and Parmesan Cheese Appetizer Ribeye Dipped in Blue Cheese Butter	4 **5PM:** Ribeye Dipped in Blue Cheese Butterfoie gras+ Home made french fries fried in duck fat or Tallow	5 **5PM:** Ribeye Dipped in Blue Cheese Butter **5:30PM:** 1 Large Scoop Kiltz's Ice Cream	6 **5PM:** Ribeye Dipped in Blue Cheese Butter	7 **5PM:** Ribeye Dipped in Blue Cheese Butter with 3oz duck liver foie gras	8 **5PM:** Ribeye Dipped in Blue Cheese Butter
9 **5PM:** Ribeye Dipped in Blue Cheese Butter	10 **5PM:** Ribeye Dipped in Blue Cheese Butter	11 **5PM:** Ribeye Dipped in Blue Cheese Butter	12 **5PM:** Ribeye Dipped in Blue Cheese Butter **5:30PM:** 1 Large Scoop Kiltz's Ice Cream	13 **5PM:** Ribeye Dipped in Blue Cheese Butter	14 **5PM:** Ribeye Dipped in Blue Cheese Butter with 3oz duck liver foie gras	15 **5PM:** Ribeye Dipped in Blue Cheese Butter 5oz side of pork belly
16 **5PM:** Ribeye Dipped in Blue Cheese Butter	17 **5PM:** Salami and Parmesan Cheese Appetizer Ribeye Dipped in Blue Cheese Butter	18 **2PM:** Chocolate Chip that pregnant Patient Bring in to celebrate **5PM:** Ribeye Dipped in Blue Cheese Butter	19 **5PM:** Ribeye Dipped in Blue Cheese Butter **5:30PM:** 1 Large Scoop Kiltz's Ice Cream	20 **5PM:** Ribeye Dipped in Blue Cheese Butter	21 **5PM:** Ribeye Dipped in Blue Cheese Butter with 3oz duck liver foie gras	22 **5PM:** Ribeye Dipped in Blue Cheese Butter
23 **5PM:** Ribeye Dipped in Blue Cheese Butter **5:30PM:** 1 Large Scoop Kiltz's Ice Cream	24 **5PM:** Ribeye Dipped in Blue Cheese Butter	25 **5PM:** Ribeye Dipped in Blue Cheese Butter	26 **5PM:** Ribeye Dipped in Blue Cheese Butter **5:30PM:** 1 Large Scoop Kiltz's Ice Cream	27 2PM Salami/ Prosciutto and Cheese Snack **5PM:** Ribeye Dipped in Blue Cheese Butter	28 **5PM:** Ribeye Dipped in Blue Cheese Butter with 3oz duck liver foie gras	29 **5PM:** Ribeye Dipped in Blue Cheese Butter + 5oz side of pork belly
30 **5PM:** Ribeye Dipped in Blue Cheese Butter	31 **5PM:** Ribeye Dipped in Blue Cheese Butter	1	2	3	4	5

Carnivore Meal　Kiltz's Treats　Carnivore Friendly Treats　Carnivore Break

Month 2

DR. KILTZ PERSONAL 90-DAY MEAL PLAN

SUNDAY	MONDAY	TUESDAY	WEDNESDAY	THURSDAY	FRIDAY	SATURDAY
29	30	1 **5PM:** Ribeye Dipped in Blue Cheese Butter	2 **5PM:** Ribeye Dipped in Blue Cheese Butter **5:30PM:** 1 Large Scoop Kiltz's Ice Cream	3 **5PM:** Ribeye Dipped in Blue Cheese Butter	4 **5PM:** Ribeye Dipped in Blue Cheese Butter foie gras+ Home made french fries fried in duck fat or Tallow	5 **5PM:** Ribeye Dipped in Blue Cheese Butter
6 **5PM:** Ribeye Dipped in Blue Cheese Butter **5:30PM:** 1 Large Scoop Kiltz's Ice Cream	7 **5PM:** Salami and Parmesan Cheese Appetizer Ribeye Dipped in Blue Cheese Butter	8 **5PM:** Ribeye Dipped in Blue Cheese Butterfoie gras+ Home made french fries fried in duck fat or Tallow	9 **5PM:** Ribeye Dipped in Blue Cheese Butter **5:30PM:** 1 Large Scoop Kiltz's Ice Cream	10 **5PM:** Ribeye Dipped in Blue Cheese Butter	11 **5PM:** Ribeye Dipped in Blue Cheese Butter with 3oz duck liver foie gras	12 **5PM:** Ribeye Dipped in Blue Cheese Butter
13 **5PM:** Ribeye Dipped in Blue Cheese Butter	14 **5PM:** Ribeye Dipped in Blue Cheese Butter	15 **5PM:** Ribeye Dipped in Blue Cheese Butter	16 **5PM:** Ribeye Dipped in Blue Cheese Butter **5:30PM:** 1 Large Scoop Kiltz's Ice Cream	17 **5PM:** Ribeye Dipped in Blue Cheese Butter	18 **5PM:** Ribeye Dipped in Blue Cheese Butter with 3oz duck liver foie gras	19 **5PM:** Ribeye Dipped in Blue Cheese Butter 5oz side of pork belly
20 **5PM:** Ribeye Dipped in Blue Cheese Butter	21 **5PM:** Salami and Parmesan Cheese Appetizer Ribeye Dipped in Blue Cheese Butter	22 **2PM:** Dark Chocolate **5PM:** Ribeye Dipped in Blue Cheese Butter	23 **5PM:** Ribeye Dipped in Blue Cheese Butter **5:30PM:** 1 Large Scoop Kiltz's Ice Cream	24 **5PM:** Ribeye Dipped in Blue Cheese Butter	25 **5PM:** Ribeye Dipped in Blue Cheese Butter with 3oz duck liver foie gras	26 **5PM:** Ribeye Dipped in Blue Cheese Butter
27 **5PM:** Ribeye Dipped in Blue Cheese Butter **5:30PM:** 1 Large Scoop Kiltz's Ice Cream	28 **5PM:** Ribeye Dipped in Blue Cheese Butter	29 **5PM:** Ribeye Dipped in Blue Cheese Butter	30 **5PM:** Ribeye Dipped in Blue Cheese Butter **5:30PM:** 1 Large Scoop Kiltz's Ice Cream	31 2PM Salami/ Prosciutto and Cheese Snack **5PM:** Ribeye Dipped in Blue Cheese Butter	1	2

Carnivore Meal Kiltz's Treats Carnivore Friendly Treats Carnivore Break

Month 3

DR. KILTZ PERSONAL 90-DAY MEAL PLAN

SUNDAY	MONDAY	TUESDAY	WEDNESDAY	THURSDAY	FRIDAY	SATURDAY
27	28	29	30	31	1 **5PM:** Ribeye Dipped in Blue Cheese Butter with 3oz duck liver foie gras	2 **5PM:** Ribeye Dipped in Blue Cheese Butter
3 **5PM:** Ribeye Dipped in Blue Cheese Butter **5:30PM:** 1 Large Scoop Kiltz's Ice Cream	4 **5PM:** Salami and Parmesan Cheese Appetizer Ribeye Dipped in Blue Cheese Butter	5 **5PM:** Ribeye Dipped in Blue Cheese Butterfoie gras+ Home made french fries fried in duck fat or Tallow	6 **5PM:** Ribeye Dipped in Blue Cheese Butter **5:30PM:** 1 Large Scoop Kiltz's Ice Cream	7 **5PM:** Ribeye Dipped in Blue Cheese Butter	8 **5PM:** Ribeye Dipped in Blue Cheese Butter with 3oz duck liver foie gras	9 **5PM:** Ribeye Dipped in Blue Cheese Butter
10 **5PM:** Ribeye Dipped in Blue Cheese Butter	11 **5PM:** Ribeye Dipped in Blue Cheese Butter	12 **5PM:** Ribeye Dipped in Blue Cheese Butter	13 **5PM:** Ribeye Dipped in Blue Cheese Butter **5:30PM:** 1 Large Scoop Kiltz's Ice Cream	14 **5PM:** Ribeye Dipped in Blue Cheese Butter	15 **5PM:** Ribeye Dipped in Blue Cheese Butter with 3oz duck liver foie gras	16 **5PM:** Ribeye Dipped in Blue Cheese Butter 5oz side of pork belly
17 **5PM:** Ribeye Dipped in Blue Cheese Butter	18 **5PM:** Salami and Parmesan Cheese Appetizer Ribeye Dipped in Blue Cheese Butter	19 **2PM:** Dark Chlocolate **5PM:** Ribeye Dipped in Blue Cheese Butter	20 **5PM:** Ribeye Dipped in Blue Cheese Butter **5:30PM:** 1 Large Scoop Kiltz's Ice Cream	21 **5PM:** Ribeye Dipped in Blue Cheese Butter	22 **5PM:** Ribeye Dipped in Blue Cheese Butter with 3oz duck liver foie gras	23 **5PM:** Ribeye Dipped in Blue Cheese Butter
24 **5PM:** Ribeye Dipped in Blue Cheese Butter **5:30PM:** 1 Large Scoop Kiltz's Ice Cream	25 **5PM:** Ribeye Dipped in Blue Cheese Butter	26 **5PM:** Ribeye Dipped in Blue Cheese Butter	27 **5PM:** Ribeye Dipped in Blue Cheese Butter **5:30PM:** 1 Large Scoop Kiltz's Ice Cream	28 2PM Salami/ Prosciutto and Cheese Snack **5PM:** Ribeye Dipped in Blue Cheese Butter	29 **5PM:** Ribeye Dipped in Blue Cheese Butter with 3oz duck liver foie gras	30 **5PM:** Ribeye Dipped in Blue Cheese Butter + 5oz side of pork belly
31 **5PM:** Ribeye Dipped in Blue Cheese Butter	1	2	3	4	5	6

Carnivore Meal Kiltz's Treats Carnivore Friendly Treats Carnivore Break

OMAD with Variety

BEBBIS WEEKLY MEAL PLAN

	DAY 1	DAY 2	DAY 3	DAY 4	DAY 5	DAY 6	DAY 7
Midnight	23- hour fast	23- hour fast	23- hour fast	23- hour fast	23- hour fast	23- hour fast	23- hour fast
12 PM	Ribeye Steak and Eggs + Raw Oysters	Eggs and Bacon+ Salmon pan-fried basted with butter	80/20 ground beef covered in butter and sour cream+ soft boiled eggs	Braised Pork Belly + Raw Oysters	Picanha Steak with blue cheese butter + Duck Liver Foie Gras	Prosciutto and Cheese Charcuterie + Rack of Lam dipped in own fat drippings and Butter	Beef Short Ribs+ Prawns/ Shrimp dipped in butter
Midnight	fast	fast	fast	fast	fast	fast	fast

Variety 16 Hour Fast Window (2 meals)

BEBBIS WEEKLY MEAL PLAN

	DAY 1	DAY 2	DAY 3	DAY 4	DAY 5	DAY 6	DAY 7
Midnight	fast	fast	fast	fast	fast	fast	fast
12 PM	Ribeye Steak and Eggs	Eggs and Salmon Pan-Fried Basted with Tallowe	Roasted Pork Ribs	80z. Pork belly	8 oz. Prawns with Butter and 2 Eggs	Pork Ribs and Eggs	Pork Belly
Dinner	Lamb Chops and Raw Oysters	Beef Burger with Tallow	Prawns with Tallow	Beef Burger with Tallow and Raw Oysters	8 oz. Ribeye Steak with Tallow	Lamb Chops with Tallow	Salmon Roasted with Tallow
Midnight	fast	fast	fast	fast	fast	fast	fast

Variety 20 hour Fast Window (1 meal+ 1 Snack)

BEBBIS WEEKLY MEAL PLAN

	DAY 1	DAY 2	DAY 3	DAY 4	DAY 5	DAY 6	DAY 7
Midnight	fast	fast	fast	fast	fast	fast	fast
2 PM	Prosciutto+ Cheese	Salami	Last Night Steak	Soft/ Hard Boiled Egg	Last Night Steak	Salami+ Cheese	Butter
5 PM Meal	NY Strip Dipped in Pan Drippings and Butter	Chuck Roast Dipped in Pan Drippings and Butter	Salmon Basted with and Dipped in Butter	Ribeye Steak Dipped in Blue Cheese Butter	Pork Jowel+ Oysters	80/20 or 70/30 Ground Beef with Melted Cheese, Butter and Sour Cream+ Soft Boiled Egg	Lamb Rib Chops Dipped in Pan Drippings and Butter+ Duck Liver
Midnight	fast	fast	fast	fast	fast	fast	fast

OMAD BUDGET MEAL PLAN

	DAY 1	DAY 2	DAY 3	DAY 4	DAY 5	DAY 6	DAY 7
Midnight	23- hour fast	23- hour fast	23- hour fast	23- hour fast	23- hour fast	23- hour fast	23- hour fast
12 PM	80/20 Ground Beef with Butter and Sour Cream + Eggs	Chicken Wings Tossed in Butter + Sardines	80/20 ground beef with Butter+ Cheese + soft boiled eggs	Chicken Wings Tossed in Butter	Bacon + Eggs	Crispy Pork Belly+ Canned Oysters	80/20 Ground Beef with Butter+ Cheese+ Eggs
Midnight	fast	fast	fast	fast	fast	fast	fast

Chapter Three

10 REASONS WHY BEBBIS IS THE BEST

Why is this group of foods so effective at reducing inflammation, reducing blood glucose, and generally improving health? **There is a plethora of reasons.**

Eliminates Sugar

Look at the nutritional breakdown of any food in the **BEBBIS Diet** and you'll notice a common thread: **no sugar.** Without the added sugars of most processed foods and the natural sugars found in fruits and vegetables, **BEBBIS. removes a critical source of inflammation.**

By focusing on fatty animal foods, the BEBBIS way of eating turns off the chronic stream of glucose that we get from a high-carb standard American Diet.

Our ancestors only encountered sugar sporadically when seasonal fruits were ripe. Our constant intake of plant-food carbs and toxins is highly misaligned with our physiology.

Sugar destroys a delicate membrane surrounding all our cells called the glycocalyx that plays a key role in immune health and numerous critical bodily functions and it promotes the harmful binding of sugar molecules to healthy tissues in a process called glycation.

By turning off the steady stream of sugar, you protect your body from chronic cell and tissue damage associated with:

- Reduced immune system strength
- Kidney failure
- Eye damage and other complications of diabetes
- Diseases such as PCOS and insulin resistance
- High blood pressure
- Progressive heart disease
- Cancer metastasis and resistance to chemotherapy
- Inflammatory diseases (including autoimmune diseases, bowel disorders, osteoporosis, infertility, and more)
- Type 2 diabetes
- Epithelial cell cancers

Eliminates Antinutrients

In addition to toxins explicitly designed to harm predators, plants also contain compounds that, when consumed by humans, act as antinutrients. Antinutrients get their name because they interfere with digestive enzymes and bind to minerals leading to nutritional deficiencies. minerals leading to nutritional deficiencies.

Eliminates Seed Oils

A BEBBIS approach to eating completely eliminates industrial seed "vegetable oils"– some of the unhealthiest "foods" ever invented. Numerous studies tell us that the modern turn towards industrial vegetable oils is a driving force behind heart disease, various cancers, and inflammatory and metabolic disorders.

Vegetable and seed oils have been shown to cause:

- Oxidative stress
- Inflammation
- Mitochondrial dysfunction
- Genetic damage

Studies show that only morbid obesity and heavy smoking are more deadly than vegetable oil. Since we know that consuming vegetable oil is a key driver in obesity, it is safe to say that vegetable oil is actually the most dangerous lifestyle factor on earth. In fact, Dr. Kiltz believes that it isn't unhealthy to be obese, it is unhealthy to be eating the foods in such quantities that typically lead to obesity and that their health is dramatically improved with dietary changes far before any weight is lost.

Increased Risk of Death by Diet/Lifestyle Factor

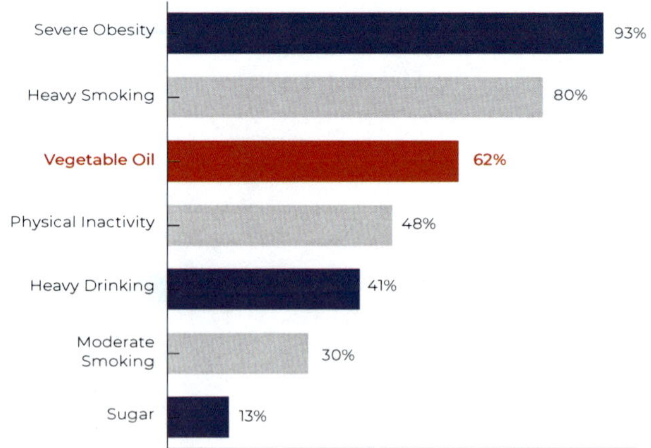

Eliminates Plant Toxins

Most people aren't familiar with plant toxins or really the fact that they exist at all. We can thank the pervasive plant-based nutritional establishment for that.

The truth is plants (just like animals) don't want to be eaten. They want to survive and reproduce to ensure the survival of their species. What they lack in animal defenses like claws, teeth, and feet, they make up for in an arsenal of chemical plant defense mechanisms.

Plants use an array of toxins to fend off predators, and, in many instances, to drive down their populations by using phytohormones to make them infertile!

Researchers estimate that humans consuming plant foods ingest around 1.5 grams of natural pesticides every day. That works out to 10,000 times more natural pesticides than synthetic compounds.

Plant toxins contribute to an all too common condition called intestinal permeability or "leaky gut," which promotes chronic inflammation and autoimmune disorders.

By eliminating most plant foods, the BEBBIS Diet protects you from the following plant toxins:

Common plant toxins and antinutrients include:

- Lectins
- Saponins
- Tannins
- Glycoalkaloids
- Glucosinolates
- Sulforaphane
- Oxalates
- Phenols
- Salicylates
- Cyanogenic glycosides
- Trypsin inhibitors
- Isoflavones and phyto hormones
- Photosensitizers
- Omega-6 fatty acids
- Mold

Destructive plant antigens—naturally occurring vegetable compounds that attack healthy human cells—along with glucose from plants get micronized in our gut and deposited through the bloodstream to every organ in our bodies, leading to widespread inflammation.

Plant toxins and antinutrients are frequently the culprits behind digestive disorders, headaches, asthma, joint pain, and other allergic responses associated with food sensitivities and various inflammatory autoimmune diseases.

Our primate ancestors evolved into humans by leaving plants behind and consuming a diet of fatty meats. Our bodies are physiologically primed to thrive on meat, while we've lost the ability to safely digest plant foods.

Chemical	Effect	Plant Group
Alkaloids	· Damages carb and fat metabolism · Damages DNA Repai · Damages nerve transmission	Nightshades like tomatoes, eggplants, potatoes
Cyanogenic glycosides	· Releases Neurotoxic cyanide-activated upon tissue damage · Disrupts normal thyroid function	Cherries, peaches, tapiocam corn, lima beans, almonds, over 2,500 plant species
Lectins (gluten) & Saponins	· Causes leaky gut · Inflammation · Autoimmunity · Cellular communication breakdown	Wheat (WGA), legumes, beans, peas, lentils, zucchini, peanuts
Phenolics, Tannins, & Photosensitizers	· Liver and Kidney Damage · Zinc and Iron Metal deficiency · Light sensitivity · Blistering and Lesions	Legumes, chocolate, wine, coffee, vinegar, celery, carrots, wild parsnip
Phytic Acid	· Reduces mineral absorption, like zinc, iron and calcium	Grains, seeds, nuts, potatoes
Sulforaphane	· Induces cancer cell death · Poisons mitochondria, kills healthy cells, generates reactive oxygen species	Cruciferous Veggies: Broccoli, cauliflower, brussels sprouts, arugula
Oxolates	· Reduces calcium and magnesium absorption · Kidney Stones	Grains, nuts, soy, spinach, chocolate, black tea

It's Affordable

Fat has twice as many calories per gram as either protein or carbs. This means that when you're eating a fatty BEBBIS meal, you're actually eating less food by weight while getting a superior return on investment. Animal foods are also much higher in bioavailable micronutrients–so you simply don't need to eat as much stuff. It's all there in these foods that are perfectly designed by nature to fuel our bodies.

When you're satiated from whole animal foods there's no need to waste money on nutrient-hollow snacks. And when you're eliminating nearly all plant foods, you're also dramatically reducing food waste. The average American throws away $1,600 in produce each year! That's enough for a lot of delicious ribeye steaks.

Eliminates Dietary Fiber

The BEBBIS diet calls for a drastic reduction in fiber. For most of us raised with the belief that we can't poop without fiber; that we need it to reduce cholesterol and to keep our bowels clean and healthy, this can be a difficult one to process. So let's let the science speak for itself.

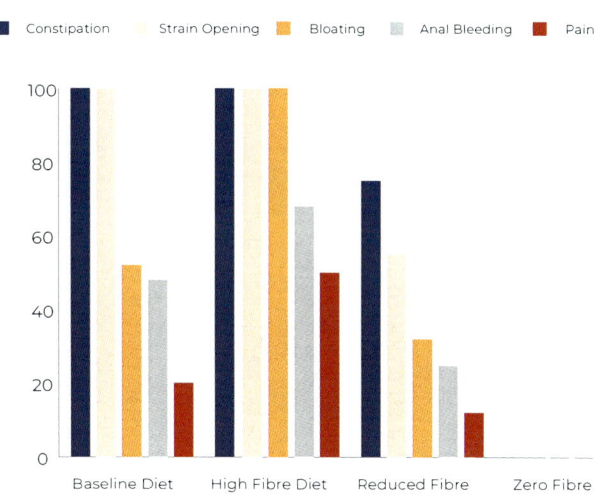

The fact is modern research is telling us that dietary fiber is wholly unnecessary and likely harmful. Researchers did not mince their words in this 2012 study published in the World Journal of Gastroenterology. They stated, "the previous strongly-held belief that the application of dietary fiber to help constipation is but a myth. Our study shows a very strong correlation between improving constipation and its associated symptoms after stopping dietary fiber intake."

A 2007 randomized control trial found that eliminating fiber for as little as two weeks leads to significant reductions in symptoms of IBS and constipation. The idea that fiber is more detrimental than beneficial makes sense in the context of our ancestral dietary evolution. **Our cavemen ancestors evolved on a diet of mainly fatty meat for nearly two million years.**

It's Simple and Easy to Follow

BEBBIS is incredibly easy to follow. It simplifies shopping, cooking, and eating. The foods are so nutrient-rich that you'll need to eat fewer types of food less often, while ending each feast feeling completely satiated. Eating one or two BEBBIS meals a day frees up time, energy, and mental space to focus on every other aspect of life like your relationships, connecting with nature and creativity, personal growth, and career goals.

PRIME RIBEYE 1LB

8 Nutrients found only in meat

1. B12
2. D3
3. DHA
4. Heme Iron
5. Carnitine
6. Carnosine
7. Creatine
8. Taurine

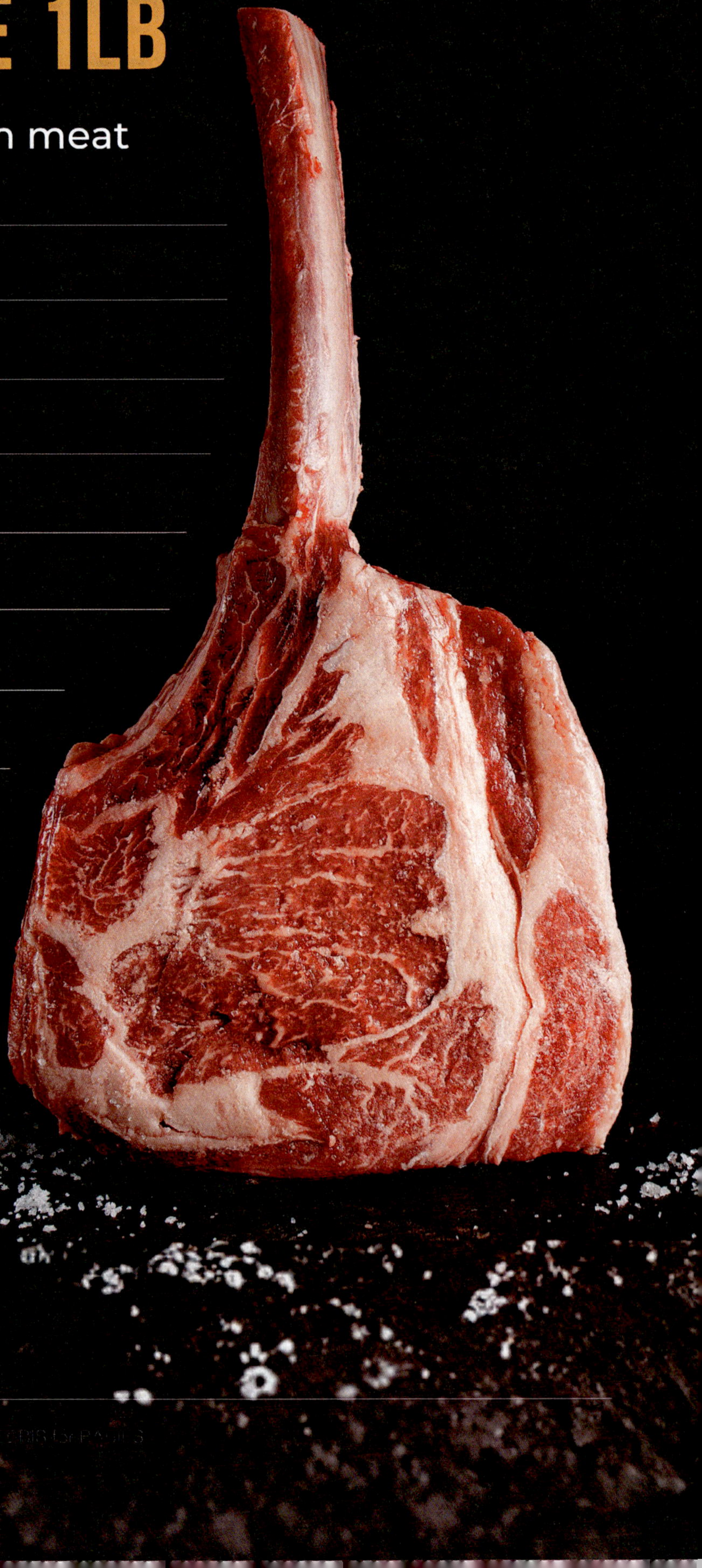

Nourishes the Body with the most nutrient dense foods on earth.

Animal foods are the most nutrient-dense and healthiest foods in the world. They offer an abundance of every macro and micronutrient your body needs to thrive. And they're free from non-essential carbs, plant toxins and antinutrients.

The idea that animal foods are healthy can come as a shock to most of us raised in a society where meat has been disparaged since the 1960s. But modern research is telling us that the demonization of meat is totally unfounded and has been one of the most catastrophic public health directives in human history.

- **Total meat consumption corre lates to greater life expectancy,** independent of the competing effects of total calorie intake, economic affluence, urban advantages, and obesity
- Saturated fat when consumed as part of a matrix of whole foods including fresh meat, is healthy

Ribeye steak and other fatty ruminant meats are chock full of healthy fats, B vitamins, zinc, selenium, and various nutrients only found in meat:

- **Carnitine:** supports male fertility, mitochondrial function, supports heart health and fertility
- **Taurine:** This antioxidant can reduce glycation, reduce oxidative stress, and improve mental health
- **Carnosine:** Supports heart health, reduces glycation, and protects telomeres for anti-aging benefits
- **Creatine:** improves cognition and protects against neurodegeneration. Supports athletic performance, and heart health

Nutritional Comparison of Beef to Other Super Foods

	Beef	Egg	Beef Liver	Kale	Blueberries
Calories	274	167	175	50.0	57.0
Carbohydrates	0.0 g	2.2 g	5.2 g	10.0 g	14.5 g
Protein	17.5 g	1.7 g	26.5 g	24.4 mg	0.7 g
Total Fat	22.1 g	12.2 g	4.7 g	0.7 g	0.3 g
Vitamin A	0.0 IU	526 IU	26091 IU	15376 IU	54.0 IU
Vitamin C	0.0 mg	0.2 mg	0.7 mg	120 mg	9.7 mg
Vitamin D	7 IU	34.0 IU	19 IU	—	—
Vitamin E	—	1.1 mg	.5 mg	—	0.6 mg
Vitamin K	—	4.0 mcg	3.9 mcg	817 mcg	19.3 mcg
Thiamin	0.1 mg	0.1 mg	0.2 mg	0.1 mg	0.0 mg
Niacin	3.2 mg	0.1 mg	17.5 mg	1.0 mg	0.4 mg
Vitamin B6	0.4 mg	0.1 mg	1.0 mg	0.3 mg	0.1 mg
Folate	5.0 mcg	30.0 mcg	26.0 mcg	29.0 mcg	6.0 mcg
Vitamin B12	3.1 mcg	0.8 mcg	83.1 mcg	0.0 mcg	0.0 mcg
Calcium	10.0 mg	71.0 mg	6 mg	135 mg	6.0 mg
Iron	1.9 mg	1.2 mg	36.2 mg	1.7 mg	0.3 mg
Magnesium	18.0 mg	12.0 mg	22 mg	34.0 mg	6.0 mg
Potassium	305 mg	138 mg	351 mg	447 mg	77.0 mg
Sodium	56.0 mg	280 mg	77.0 mg	43.0 mg	1.0 mg
Zinc	3.8 mg	1.0 mg	5.2 mg	0.4 mg	0.2 mg

Eliminates Bacteria

A BEBBIS diet that eliminates most plant foods protects us from exposure to ubiquitous toxins both within and on the outside of plants.

Studies show that alarmingly high percentages of plant foods are contaminated with protecting harmful bacteria like listeria, E. coli, and Klebsiella.

A 2016 study that examined 105 samples of imported fresh fruits and vegetables found that **60% of fruits and 91% of vegetables carried potentially harmful bacteria.**

- 20% of fruits and 42% of vegetables had Enterococcus.
- 22% of fruits and 7% of vegetables had E. coli and S. aureus
- 21 other species of bacteria were identified with E. coli, Klebsiella pneumoniae, Enterococcus casse liflavus, and Enterobacter cloacae as the most abundant species.

A 2021 review found that "raw consumption of many fresh leafy and non-leafy vegetables, root vegetables, sprouts, and fruits results in the exposure of humans to foodborne bacterial pathogens, including antibiotic-resistant bacteria (ARB). In recent decades, exposure to antimicrobial-resistant pathogens through the food chain has increasingly been reported to cause foodborne disease outbreaks.

The presence of ARB (antibiotic resistance bacteria) and ARGs (antimicrobial resistance genes) in fresh produce and salads consumed raw poses potential public health risks of unknown magnitude. Preventing ARB/ARG exposure through fresh produce may be challenging considering the cross-cutting issues related to food security and food safety..."

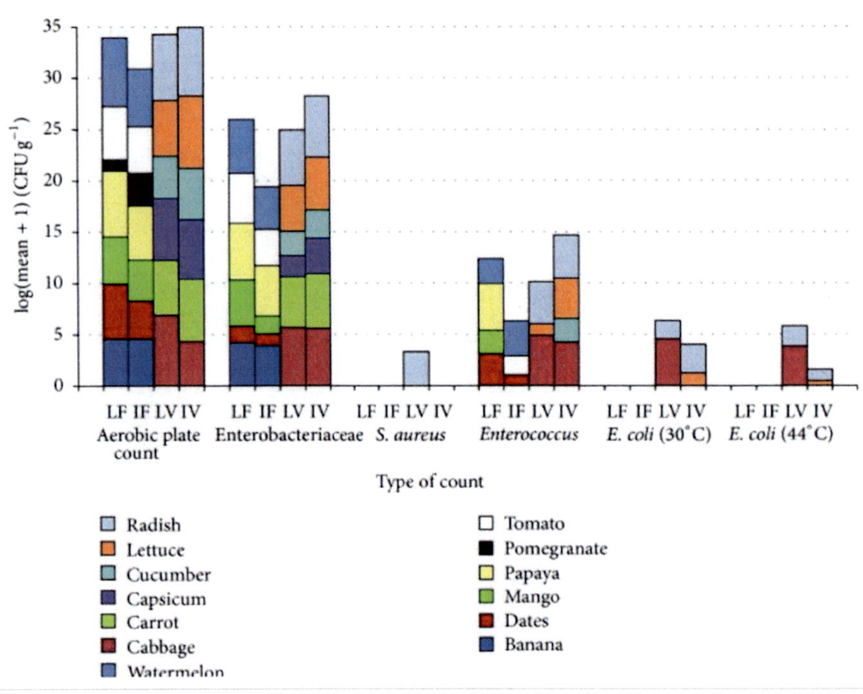

Harnesses the Benefits of Intermittent Feasting

Dr. Kiltz calls intermittent fasting by its more accurate term, "feasting". It's another feature of ancestral eating patterns that we can apply to our modern lifestyle to optimize our health and wellness. Our ancestors didn't have refrigeration, so they had to feast on their prey when it was fresh. Then between successful hunts, they fasted. Over eons, our bodies and brains adapted to this pattern as a metabolically optimal rhythm.

We see this reflected in modern research that reveals how we have better cognitive function during times of food scarcity. **And our cognitive ability diminishes when we don't fast.** Other intermittent fasting research shows how adopting this ancestral fasting/feasting pattern to our modern lives can offer numerous health benefits including:

- Restoring gut health
- Blood sugar regulation
- Cholesterol and triglycerides control
- Supports heart health
- Increased lean muscle mass
- Stimulates human growth hormone
- Stem cell production
- Supports mindful eating habits

There are a lot of different intermittent fasting methods, and all of them can be effective. Dr. Kiltz recommends **OMAD,** which stands for **"One Meal a Day"** as the ideal method for BEBBIS. Practicing OMAD consistently trains your body to rest and digest at the same time every day. Eating right after sundown will also allow you to take advantage of the benefits of circadian rhythm fasting.

With OMAD, it's important to eat enough–and that's where BEBBIS comes in. These foods are extremely nutrient-dense and efficient, while also being incredibly delicious.

Chapter Four

30-DAYS TO CARNIVORE

INTRODUCTION TO CARNIVORE

Transitioning to a carnivore lifestyle—whether you go cold turkey or in stages—takes planning and commitment. We advise our soon-to-be BEBBIS moms and dads to use the first week to shop, clear out your pantry and refrigerator, read through all of the menus, shopping lists, recipes, and fully commit.

Get Inspired: Read motivational carnivore stories from folks who have successfully adapted to carnivore eating. We've shared a few here. You'll see stories of weight loss, improved energy, reduced inflammation, no more brain fog, improved libido, and just plain feeling great. Many show marked improvements in egg quality and quantity and hormone levels returning to where they should be.

By focusing on where you're headed, you'll have the energy and willpower to clean out your pantry, stock up on carnivore essentials, and plan for the weeks ahead.

Clean Out: If you've been considering the switch to carnivore, it's likely you've already decreased the number of carbohydrates and processed foods you have on hand. If not, now is the time to go through your kitchen pantry and remove any foods listed in the **FOODS TO ELIMINATE chart.** Donate unopened cans or boxes to a food bank/pantry. Carnivore is a streamlined diet. You'll find you have a lot more room in your pantry and refrigerator, but you may need extra freezer space for meats!

Stock Up: Order eggs, meats, and butter/tallow from local supplier/farmers or ones that we've recommended. Subscriptions and bulk purchases are a convenient way to save and ensure you always have an easy meal on hand.

Be Prepared: Be prepared to have a few challenging days early on when you don't feel all that great, you're tempted (or even cheated), and doubting carnivore. Be patient, stick to it, and you'll be through the adjustment phase before you know it. Follow some of our tips to reduce adjustment symptoms and consider joining a carnivore group like Kiltz Mighty Tribe with other like-minded carnivores who can offer tips, ideas, and support.

Be Patient: With yourself and others who may not understand the why, what, and how of your carnivore decision. By following our TIPS TO SUCCEED, you'll be on your way to a new Carnivore you!

CARNIVORE IN REAL LIFE
SUSTAINABILITY HACKS

When you are invited to a social event or holiday party, it may seem impossible to stick to your goals. It is totally possible for you to live a normal social life while maintaining boundaries around your health and wellness.

SOCIAL

Tip 1: Have a specific goal with a deadline. It is so much easier to stick to your goals when you have a goal to stick to.

Tip 2: If you are not the host, inform the host of your dietary restrictions. This will help prevent awkwardness day-of.

Tip 3: Eat before you go If your'e uncomfortable or just don't feel like explaining your diet to others, this can save you from having to explain.

Tip 4: If you are making dishes for the meal, make your favorite carnivore meals!

Tip 5: Provide your own dietary options for every stage of the meal. This is a great opportunity for a magnificent charcuterie board! You can also plan on taking an additional meat side to share.

If you do eat something that does not meet your nutritional goals, **forgive yourself and keep moving forward.** and remeber progress over perfection. You are human!

CARNIVORE SNACKS

Purchase While Traveling

Whisps, Jerky, Beef Sticks, Cheese Sticks, Pork Rinds, Eggs, fully cooked bacon/ sausages

Pack Ahead of Time

Bacon, Prepped Meat - burgers, meatballs, meat muffins, wraps, nourish bowls, eggs, cheesesticks, canned or pouch chicken, tuna, salmon, sardines, wag bar, carnivore crisps/snacks, lunch/deli meats

DINING OUT IDEAS

Fast Food

Some of these options are not 100% ideal, but they are better than not eating carnivore at all and will allow more flexibility and therefore sustainability in your diet.

When eating out, ask for just the burger or egg, bacon and cheese in a breakfast sandwich, grilled nuggets, wings, sous vide egg bites, meat off of a catering/bbq menu, meat from inside of a taco, or just meat/cheese from a build-a-bowl/salad place.

Dining out

American fare: Chicken wings, burger patties, ask what is in their meatloaf, steak, pork chops, chicken breast

Mexican restaurant: Typically if they serve tacos you can "double your protein" so you can just order 3 sides of beef/chicken/pork, fajitas (order shrimp and beef for more volume at lower cost).

Asian restaurant: This is a great one because entrees are often separate from the carbs anyways - Mongolian beef, no sauce.

Sushi restaurant: Sashimi.

Italian restaurant: Oysters, sausages, ask what is in their meatballs, scrape the toppings off of a meat lover's pizza with no sauce.

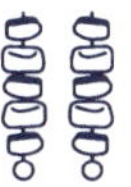

Mediterranean fare: Side of gyro meat.

Other: Restaurant options that are more carnivore friendly: BBQ, Brazilian steakhouse, normal steakhouse

SUCCESS PRINCIPLES

MENTAL PREP

To support new lifestyle changes, **it's important to understand and fully explore your motivation for wanting to change.** Take some time to reflect and use the section below to journal on your goals.

MY MOTIVATION

I want to change because:

When I change, I will feel:

I must change now because:

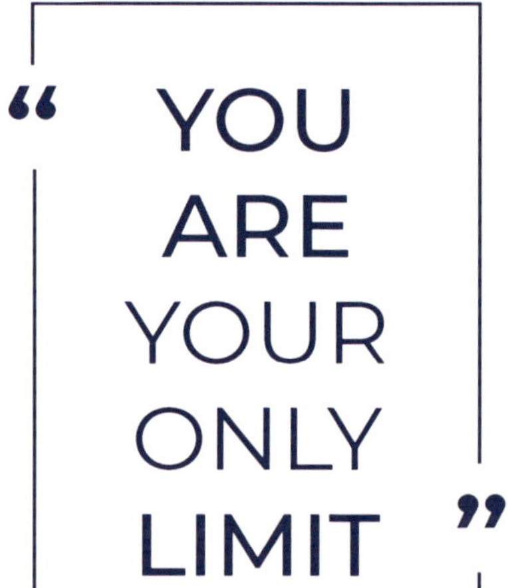

COMMIT
TO CARNIVORE AND YOURSELF

Committing to a carnivore lifestyle is demanding, but the improvements you'll experience in your physical and mental health and wellness make the challenges ahead worth the effort.

Your body will feel different.

You'll experience a range of physical symptoms during the transition, but your mind will clear.

Some days will be harder than others, and you'll need to deal with social situations where your commitment will be tested.

Commit to taking care of yourself by scheduling time to cook.

You don't need to justify how or what you choose to eat.

Persevere and know that these are bumps in the road on the way to enjoying improved health and wellness.

THE ADJUSTMENT PHASE

Change is difficult, and starting a carnivore lifestyle is no different. You're eating fewer calories (sometimes), on a different schedule, and from mainly animal sources. It takes time for your body to adjust to fewer carbs and chemicals. As you adapt to this new lifestyle, you may temporarily experience some side effects. **Here are some common side effects and how to combat them successfully:**

Adaptation Symptoms

Headaches or Migraines

Brain Fog

Lack of Energy and General Fatigue (mental and physical)

Dizziness or balance issues

Flu-like symptoms

Muscle Aches

Bad breath or metallic taste in your mouth

Sore Throat

Nausea

Diarrhea

Difficulty sleeping

Night Sweats

How to Reduce Symptoms

DRINK ENOUGH WATER & ELECTROLYTES:
Make sure you increase your water consumption and add in electrolytes (sodium, potassium, magnesium, and chloride) to make up for what you are losing in water weight. Staying hydrated can help alleviate symptoms like muscle cramps and fatigue.

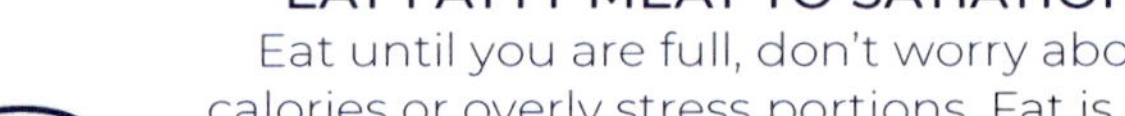

EAT FATTY MEAT TO SATIATION:
Eat until you are full, don't worry about calories or overly stress portions. Fat is your purest energy source, and eating enough of it can reduce cravings you keep you feeling satisfied. Slowly cutting back on carbs and increasing your fat intake can decrease symptoms as you transition.

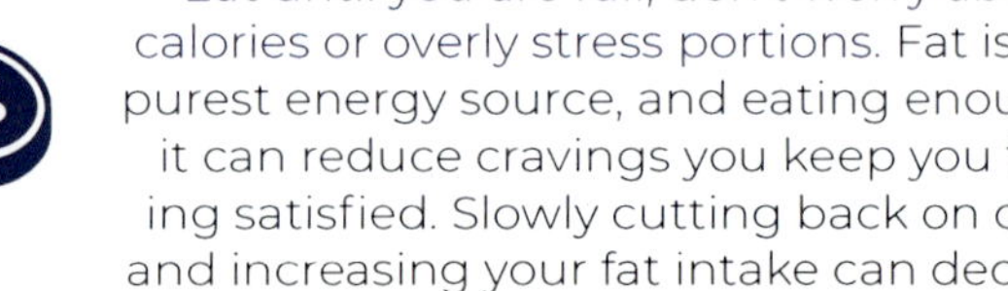

GET ADEQUATE SLEEP:
Insomnia and interrupted sleep are both common symptoms during the transition phase. Sometimes restricting water consumption just before bed and not eating during the 3-4 hours before bedtime may help prevent nighttime bathroom visits. Optimize sleep conditions by making sure your room is cool and dark, taking a bath or shower to relax, and establish a consistent schedule that you stick to 7 days a week.

BREAK A SWEAT:
Sweating is our body's natural way of detoxifying. Sweating during some light to moderate exercise can help you sleep better and cleanse the body of toxins. Avoid strenuous exercise while first adapting to the carnivore diet

CONSIDER SUPPLEMENTS:
Lipase supplements can help G.I. unrest as your body acclimates to higher fat intake. Ox Bile can also be added if Lipase doesn't appear to ease your symptoms.

*The good news is that most of these symptoms are temporary and will dissipate as your body begins to naturally adapt to the carnivore lifestyle.

TIPS TO SUCCEED

Build Routines

Structure and routine will help you stay on track and simplify the adaptation of the carnivore diet. Preparing your meals ahead of time and eating at or around the same time each day and will reduce required thinking and increase automaticity.

Find Structure and a "Schedule"

The 2 MAD eating schedule is not designed to stress the exact timing of your meals. Eat when your lifestyle dictates and when your body demands.

Eating your meals at roughly the same time each day provides the following benefits:

- Getting your digestive system in rhythm
- Maintaining sustainable energy levels
- Encouraging consistent sleep pattern
- Allowing consistent performance with training (if applicable)

Limit or Eliminate Snacking

If you are just beginning to experiment with intermittent meals and fasting then you are likely used to eating 3+ times per day. Small snacks can help to ease the hunger pains you may experience during the transitional period. **If you are going to snack, remember to keep it carnivore.** Refer to our carnivore snack guide for ideas.

Determining Portion Size

The information included in this guide constitutes a sample meal plan for you to follow. **Adjust portion sizes based on goals** (i.e. building muscle/strength, weight loss, or weight maintenance). Refer to "Tailoring the Diet to Your Goals" Guide for additional information. Portion size will also be review during the Sunday preparation for the week meetings.

Meal Prep

Absolutely not required, but is great for busy people who are looking to save time. **Meal prepping entails preparing meals ahead of time** and then portioning them out so they are ready to go each day.

Following Instructions for Meals

Follow the ingredients listed for each individual meal and the instructions as a guide when preparing food. Extra portions required for next day meals are built into the instructions and ingredients.

WEEK ONE MENU

	FAST	BREAKFAST/LUNCH	FAST	DINNER
DAY 1	COFFEE, WATER, OR ELECTROLYTES	BACON AND EGGS	WATER, OR ELECTROLYTES	RIBEYE
DAY 2	COFFEE, WATER, OR ELECTROLYTES	LEFTOVER RIBEYE (4 OZ)	WATER, OR ELECTROLYTES	SIMPLE GROUND BEEF IN TALLOW
DAY 3	COFFEE, WATER, OR ELECTROLYTES	GROUND BEEF AND 2 EGGS	WATER, OR ELECTROLYTES	SALMON ROASTED W/ TALLOW
DAY 4	COFFEE, WATER, OR ELECTROLYTES	BACON AND EGGS	WATER, OR ELECTROLYTES	RIBEYE
DAY 5	COFFEE, WATER, OR ELECTROLYTES	LEFTOVER RIBEYE (4 OZ)	WATER, OR ELECTROLYTES	PORKCHOPS
DAY 6	COFFEE, WATER, OR ELECTROLYTES	BACON AND EGGS	WATER, OR ELECTROLYTES	SIMPLE GROUND BEEF IN TALLOW
DAY 7	 COFFEE, WATER, OR ELECTROLYTES	 LEFTOVER GROUND BEEF AND EGGS	 WATER, OR ELECTROLYTES	 BACON WRAPPED TENDERLOIN & SHRIMP

SHOPPING LIST

BACON
X 1 package (12 strips)

BUTTER
5 sticks (36 tbsp) - minimum-(KerryGold, organic butter with salt, or local butter with salt)

EGGS
One dozen (carton)

GROUND BEEF
80/20 2 lbs

DICED PANCETTA
2 oz -1 package

PORK CHOPS
6 oz – x2

RIBEYE
16 oz – x2

SALMON FILET
8 oz x 1

SALT
(Redmond's or Pink Himalayan or Celtic Sea Salt)

SHRIMP
One lb cooked or raw (12 large shrimp)

TALLOW
1 package (12 tbsp) – minimum

TENDERLOIN 4 oz – x 2

NOTES
Buy butter and tallow in bulk and buy more than you think you'll need. Both will be used generously.

COOKING ESSENTIALS
Spatula
Wooden spoon
Oven proof pan/ skillet

PANTRY ESSENTIALS
Salt
Butter
Tallow

WEEK TWO MENU

	FAST	BREAKFAST/LUNCH	FAST	DINNER
DAY 1	COFFEE, WATER, OR ELECTROLYTES	BACON AND EGGS	WATER, OR ELECTROLYTES	SALMON ROASTED W/ TAL-LOW
DAY 2	 COFFEE, WATER, OR ELECTROLYTES	SALMON	WATER, OR ELECTROLYTES	 SIMPLE GROUND BEEF IN TALLOW
DAY 3	 COFFEE, WATER, OR ELECTROLYTES	GROUND BEEF AND 2 EGGS	 WATER, OR ELECTROLYTES	 CHICKEN WINGS
DAY 4	 COFFEE, WATER, OR ELECTROLYTES	PANCETTA AND EGGS	 WATER, OR ELECTROLYTES	 RIBEYE
DAY 5	 COFFEE, WATER, OR ELECTROLYTES	 LEFTOVER RIBEYE (4 OZ)	 WATER, OR ELECTROLYTES	 SALMON ROASTED W/ TALLOW
DAY 6	COFFEE, WATER, OR ELECTROLYTES	 BACON AND EGGS	 WATER, OR ELECTROLYTES	 SIMPLE GROUND BEEF IN TALLOW
DAY 7	 COFFEE, WATER, OR ELECTROLYTES	 LEFTOVER GROUND BEEF AND 2 EGGS	 WATER, OR ELECTROLYTES	 RIBEYE & SHRIMP

SHOPPING LIST

BACON
X 1 package (12 strips)

BUTTER
5 sticks (36 tbsp) - minimum-(KerryGold, organic butter with salt, or local butter with salt)

CHICKEN WINGS
1 package (minimun 10) remaining can be frozen

EGGS
One dozen (carton)

GROUND BEEF
80/20 2 lbs

DICED PANCETTA
2 oz -1 package

RIBEYE
16 oz – x1 and 12 oz x 1- 28 oz total

SALMON FILET
20 oz total

SALT
(Redmond's or Pink Himalayan or Celtic Sea Salt)

SHRIMP
One lb cooked or raw (12 large shrimp)

TALLOW
1 package (12 tbsp) – minimum

NOTES
Buy butter and tallow in bulk and buy more than you think you'll need. Both will be used generously.

COOKING ESSENTIALS
Spatula
Wooden spoon
Oven proof pan/ skillet

PANTRY ESSENTIALS
Salt
Butter
Tallow

WEEK THREE MENU

	FAST	BREAKFAST/LUNCH	FAST	DINNER
DAY 1	COFFEE, WATER, OR ELECTROLYTES	BACON AND EGGS	WATER, OR ELECTROLYTES	CARNIVORE BLUE CHEESE BURGERS
DAY 2	COFFEE, WATER, OR ELECTROLYTES	BACON AND EGGS	WATER, OR ELECTROLYTES	SALMON ROASTED W/ TALLOW
DAY 3	COFFEE, WATER, OR ELECTROLYTES	SALMON	WATER, OR ELECTROLYTES	RIBEYE
DAY 4	COFFEE, WATER, OR ELECTROLYTES	LEFTOVER RIBEYE (4 OZ)	WATER, OR ELECTROLYTES	CHICKEN WINGS
DAY 5	COFFEE, WATER, OR ELECTROLYTES	PANCETTA AND EGGS	WATER, OR ELECTROLYTES	SIMPLE GROUND BEEF W/ TALLOW
DAY 6	COFFEE, WATER, OR ELECTROLYTES	LEFTOVER GROUND BEEF AND 2 EGGS	WATER, OR ELECTROLYTES	SALMON ROASTED W/ TALLOW
DAY 7	COFFEE, WATER, OR ELECTROLYTES	BACON AND EGGS	WATER, OR ELECTROLYTES	RIBEYE & SHRIMP

SHOPPING LIST

BACON
X 1 package (12 strips)

BLUE CHEESE
1 package (minimum 50 g)

BUTTER
5 sticks (36 tbsp) - minimum- (Grass fed butter, salted butter, local butter, or clarified butter (ghee)

CHICKEN WINGS
1 package (minimun 10) remaining can be frozen

EGGS
One dozen (carton)

GROUND BEEF
80/20 2 lbs

DICED PANCETTA
2 oz -1 package

RIBEYE
28oz total- (16oz x1 &12oz x 1)

SALMON FILET
20 oz total- (12 oz x 1 & 8 oz x1)

SALT
(Redmond's or Pink Himalayan or Celtic Sea Salt)

SHRIMP
One lb cooked or raw (12 large shrimp)

TALLOW
1 package (12 tbsp) – minimum

NOTES

Buy butter and tallow in bulk and buy more than you think you'll need. Both will be used generously.

COOKING ESSENTIALS

Spatula
Wooden spoon
Oven proof pan/ skillet

PANTRY ESSENTIALS

Salt
Butter
Tallow

Chapter Five

BUYING AND COOKING MEAT

HOW TO SHOP FOR MEAT

Committing to a meat-rich diet means changing the way you shop, cook, and eat. Meats from local sources are usually the freshest and most affordable. Farmer's markets, co-ops, grocery stores or your local butcher are all good sources. To find a local farm, look at Eatwild's Directory of Farms.

This is a list of more than 1,400 pasture-based farms in the United States and Canada selling grass-fed or pastured meat and dairy products, including: Beef, Pork, Lamb, Veal, Goat, Elk, Venison, Yak, Chickens, Ducks, Rabbits, Turkeys, Eggs, Milk, Cheeses, and more.

If you're buying meat from your local grocery store or wholesale club, be sure to take advantage of sales and stock up. **Buy well-marbled steaks and 80/20 ground beef in bulk** and freeze it in the portion sizes that make sense for the way you cook.

WHAT TO LOOK FOR

Look for local, pasture-raised, grass-fed beef

Grass-fed animals have a higher fat content than grain-fed beef, which means it's more flavorful and melts in your mouth. These cattle are not only better for the environment but also produce meat that is higher in nutrients. If you can afford 100% grass-fed, of course, you should choose grass-fed meat because it has a better fatty acid profile and antioxidant content and is likely to contain a lower level of contaminants like pesticides, herbicides, and antimicrobials. But be rest assured that grain-fed meat is still one of the most nutrient-dense foods you can eat.

Look for Good Marbling

Streaks of fat throughout the muscle are called marbling. Cuts with fat are juicier and more tender after cooking. The more marbling, the more tender the meat. Ideally, choose cuts of meat that are nearly equal in grams of fat and protein. **Ask you butcher to leave your steaks untrimmed.** Steaks, roasts, and ground beef are always good choices, but ground beef often provides less fat than other cuts.

Advantages of Pasture-raised Beef

Cattle roam free on a pasture & eat only grass

- **Leaner and juicier**, thanks to higher moisture content
- **Rich in omega-3 fatty** acids, vitamin B6 & Beta-carotene
- **Richer in Conjugated linolei acid (CLA)** which improves metabolism and immunity
- **Rich in anti-oxidant** and anti-inflammatory compounds

Look for ethically sourced meat that is free from antibiotics, pesticides, and GMOs

This helps reduce your toxic load, risk of inflammation, and risk of antibiotic resistance.

COST-SAVING TIPS TO BUY MEAT

Buy cheaper, fattier meats

By choosing a lower grade of beef, you can save money. Contrary to what you might think, lower-grade beef isn't necessarily less safe or even lower quality. The USDA's grading system is based on the marbling, tenderness, and flavor of any given cut. Even the chewiest piece of beef can become melt-in-your-mouth tender if it's cooked right (low and slow is the way to go).

PRICIEST OPTION	MODERATE OPTION	CHEAPEST OPTION

Shop Around

It pays to buy in bulk for most items, and meat is no exception. Apps like Instacart are great for searching bulk deals, allowing you to compare prices of similar items across different stores. Wholesale clubs like BJs and Costco often have deals on bulk packs of ground beef, stew meat, and other cuts which can be repackaged and frozen in smaller bundles. Wholesale retailers can also be an option.

Buy a Cow Share

Many farms and butcher shops allow you to buy anywhere from a quarter-cow to a whole cow at a time, often for a steep discount. Once acquired, you can then piece your cow, store in a chest freezer, and thaw what you need each week. Whole cows can be expensive up-front, but some people find a workaround by combining their buying power with like-minded family or friends. Note that a full-share of beef can amount to around 600 pounds of beef; a quarter cow is around 150 pounds. You'll likely need to invest in a good capacity freezer to store your meat.

Shop On-line

If you can't find a local farm or store to buy from or you prefer to have your meats shipped right to your door-step, there are a variety of online providers who offer competitively priced, quality meats. Many of them offer subscription services to keep you fully stocked.

Buy Bone-In Cuts

Bone-in beef is almost always cheaper than boneless, even when you factor in the weight of the bones. Marrow bones are nutritiously valuable when it comes to making homemade bone broth.

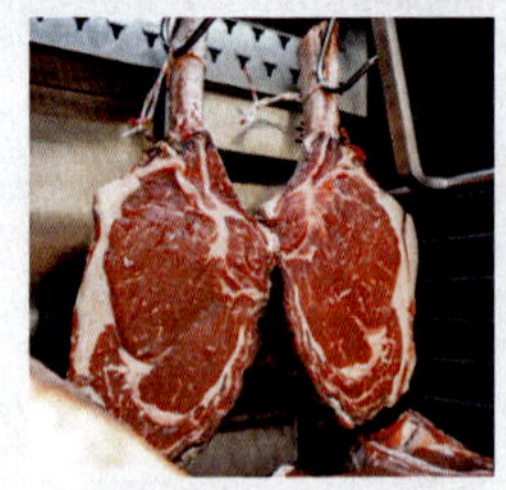

QUALITY MEAT SUPPLIERS

Snake River Farms

My go-to steak. A bit pricey, but nothing beats the incredible American wagyu of snake river farms shipped right to your door

snakeriverfarms.com

First Light Farms

Grass-fed wagyu and venison right to your door. Yup, it's damn good stuff!

firstlight.farm

Butcher Box

There's nothing like the convenience of subscription grass fed, grass finished beef and other meat products. My go to for mouth watering meats!

butcherbox.com

US Wellness Meats

My go-to steak. A bit pricey, but nothing beats the incredible American wagyu of snake river farms shipped right to your door.

grasslandbeef.com

Alpine Butcher

Online Butcher Offering USDA Prime Hand Cut Steaks For Home Delivery

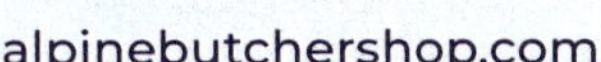
alpinebutchershop.com

Carnivore Crips

I'm usually a leftover steak in a Ziploc bag kind of guy if I need a snack or am on the road, but these crunchy yummy and nutritious snacks are well worth it!

carnivorecrisps.com

Hudson Valley Foie Gras

You can't beat Hudson Valley for delicious foie gras or duck fat. Their cage-free, responsibly raised ducks provide unbeatable flavor and nutrition.

hudsonvalleyfoiegras.com

Nose to Tail

Founded by my friend and carnivore thought leader Brian Sanders, Nose to Tail offers amazing fresh meats, beef snacks, animal-based soaps/ lotions and so much more.

nosetotail.org

Porter Road

Great high-quality meat shipped right to your door.

porterroad.com

Our Ancestor's Foods

This Florida-based family-owned business is passionate about providing customers with high-quality, grass-fed beef that is free from hormones and antibiotics.

ourancestorsfoods.com

TIPS FOR COOKING THE PERFECT RIBEYE

Choosing the Perfect Ribeye

When choosing a ribeye look for 1-1.5 inch thick cuts of meat with lots of marbling (white intramuscular fat) running through the meat.

*If you decide you want more meat, adjust accordingly. For larger ribeyes, look for 1.5 – 2 inch thick cuts.

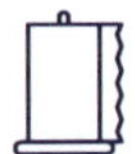

Drying Your Ribeye

Properly drying your steak allows you to **eliminate surface moisture** and is essential to ensuring a perfect sear.

To dry your ribeye, place steak on a wire rack in your fridge 1-2 days prior to cooking. Alternatively, you can simply take the ribeye out of the fridge, allow it to come to room temperature, and dry with a paper towel.

Salting Your Steak

Cover your ribeye generously in salt. Salting steaks can be done up to 48 hours before cooking (if drying overnight), 45 minutes before cooking, or immediately before cooking. Avoid salting steaks 10-25 minutes before cooking as this will cause meat to cook gray and rubbery.

Using a Meat thermometer

When it's time to check the temperature insert the thermometer THROUGH THE SIDE of the ribeye into the thickest part away from the bone, fat, and grizzle.

The sensing area of thermometers is ½ inch to 2 inches long, so this area must be completely inserted into the thickest, center area of the steak.

Resting Ribeye

After removing ribeye from the pan, oven or grill, **place ribeye onto a plate,** add additional butter if desired, cover loosely with tin foil and allow them to rest for 5-10 minutes before slicing. Resting your steak will ensure it is juicy and succulent.

Steak Doness Guide

Cook times will depend greatly on the thickness of your steak.

	Remove from heat at this temperature	Final Cooked Temperature
RARE: Cool-to-warm red center, and soft, tender texture.	118F	120F
MEDIUM RARE: Warm red center – perfect steak texture with a nice brown crust..	125F	130F
MEDIUM: steak will have a hot pink center and slightly firmer texture.	136F	140F
MEDIUM WELL	143F	150F
WELL DONE	154F	160F

HOW TO COOK RIBEYE

Ingredients

 12 oz Ribeye 1-1.5 inches thick

 Salted Butter

 Salt -kosher, pink Himalayan, Redmond's are all great (coarse salt works best)

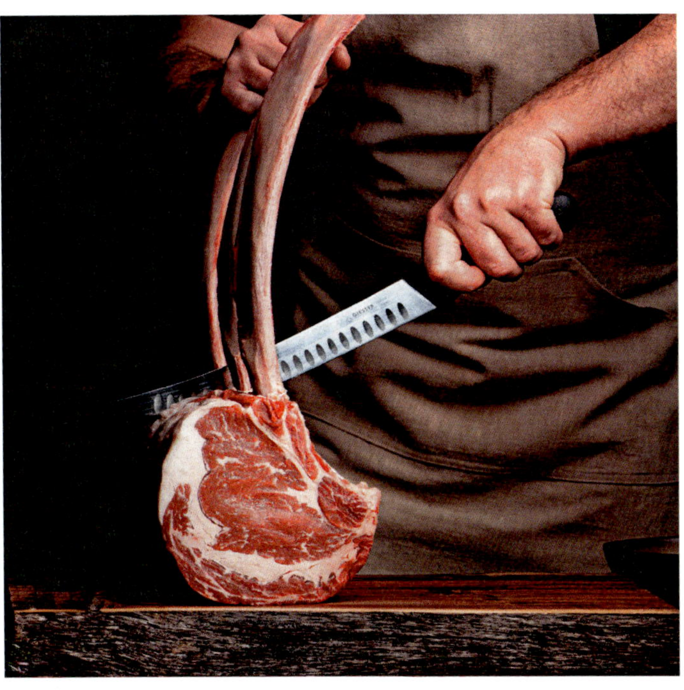

PREP

Remove steak from the fridge and allow 30-40mins for the steak to come to room temperature.

Pat all sides of steak dry with a paper towel.

Salt generously (preferably with rock salt) on all sides.

COOKING OPTIONS

In the skillet/cast iron pan

Required equipment

 Medium skillet (cast iron preferred)

 Meat thermometer

Instructions

- Heat a medium cast iron skillet over medium high heat. After 1-2 minutes, add enough butter to cover the base of the pan. Allow pan to continue heating.
- Place prepped steak in the middle of the skillet and cook, turn every 2-3 minutes, until a dark crust has formed on both sides, about 9-12 minutes.
- Reduce heat to medium low. Push steak to one side of the skillet; add butter. Cook until butter is foaming, about 30 seconds to 1 minute.
- Spoon butter over steak for 1-2 minutes, turning over once, until desired doneness.
- Let rest 5-10 minutes before slicing.

On the Grill

Required Equipment

 Gas/propane grill

 Meat thermometer - cooking steaks on the grill includes the most variables. Be sure to use your meat thermometer.

Instructions

- Preheat grill between 425° to 475°.
- Place prepped steaks on the grill. Close the lid. Flip steaks 1 minute before half way point.
- Total time for 1 inch thick steaks – rare (7-9 minutes), medium rare (9-12 minutes), Medium (12-14 minutes)
- Total time for 1.5 inch thick steaks – rare (10-12 minutes), medium rare (12-15 minutes), medium (15-17 minutes)
- Place cooked steak on a plate, cover with butter, rest for 5-10 minutes.

Chapter Six

EGGS

Egg Glossary

Regular: These are "standard" eggs and come from large commercial farm-raised chickens.

Free-range: The term "free-range" generally means the chickens for at least some part of their lives have some outdoor access.

Cage-free: Cages didn't confine the chickens. Cage-free eggs can still be produced with hens living in cramped, filthy indoor conditions.

Certified-organic: The chickens ate organic feed and weren't exposed to antibiotics or chemicals to produce certified-organic eggs.

Farm-fresh: There's not much meaning to this term and isn't any official designation. It's simply used to make customers feel "healthier" when they buy the eggs.

Kosher: Nearly all eggs are kosher. Eggs won't be kosher if broken, cracked or have blood spots in them.

Antibiotic-free: Chicken feed sometimes contains antibiotics, and some chickens receive antibiotics injections. However, antibiotic-free eggs don't have these features.

No hormones: The FDA prohibits using hormones in eggs, so all eggs fit this label. Some labels prefer to highlight this fact while others don't bother mentioning it.

Vegetarian-fed: The chickens had a strict completely vegetarian and all-organic diet. Note that chickens are omnivorous and prefer earthworms and insects along with their seeds and grains. In fact, many chickens prefer insects over plants.

Omega-3 enriched: The chickens ate an omega-3-rich diet, typically flaxseed, which is chock-full of beneficial nutrients.

Humanely raised: The chickens didn't live in cages. This term doesn't necessarily mean they had free access to sunlight and grass.

Natural: The term "natural" only means the eggs have no artificial ingredients or colors and they've experienced very little processing.

Pasture-raised: The chickens could roam their pasture freely, and the eggs came straight from these pasture-raised chickens.

Organic: Organic eggs are laid by hens who usually live in barns and have access to the sun and the outdoors. To be considered organic, hens laying organic eggs must have access to the outdoors, exercise areas, fresh air, clean drinking water, shade, and direct sunlight. "Certified organic" is a relatively reliable guarantee that "free-range" birds are managed in a healthy and humane way.

Eggs Defined

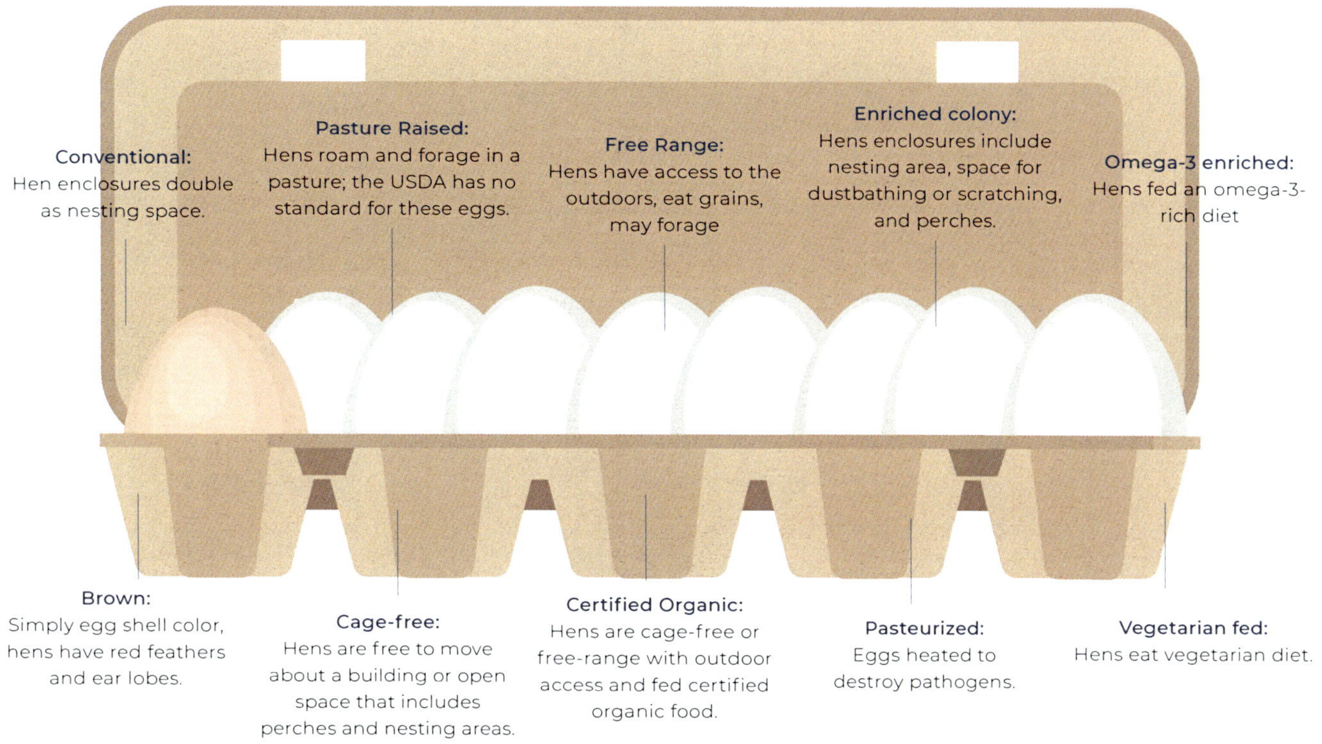

What Kind of Eggs Should I buy?

It's not at all surprising that the healthiest eggs come from the healthiest hens. But there's a ton of misinformation printed on egg cartons. Lots of phrases that sound good, but when you really dig down to what they mean, don't ensure the hens are happier or the eggs more nutritious. **Labels like hormone-free, farm-fresh, cage-free, antibiotic-free, natural, and fertile are essentially meaningless.**

An egg carton that is labeled "100% vegetarian-fed" and "cage-free" can indicate that the chickens were raised indoors in a confined space with hundreds of other chickens.

The only way to know if you have healthy eggs is by finding out how the chickens are raised. Do your research, and get to know your egg farmer if at all possible.

In addition to diet, sun exposure is a big factor in raising healthy chickens who lay nutritious eggs. Sun is a critical source of vitamin D for both humans and chickens. Vitamin D deficient hens lay eggs that have brittle shells and are less nutrient-dense.

The Best Eggs to Buy

The best eggs to buy are pasture-raised from your local farmers market or certified by third-party organizations to be organic, pasture-raised, Certified Humane or Animal Welfare Approved, and USDA grade A or AA123. These eggs have more vitamin D, omega-3 fatty acids, vitamin A, vitamin E, and beta carotene than other eggs. Omega-3 enriched and lutein-enhanced eggs are also good for health because of the extra nutrients.

Common store-bought brands that have a good reputation include:

Vital Farms, Family Homestead, Oliver's Organic, Happy Egg Co., Pete and Gerry's, Alexandre

THE HEALTHIEST WAYS TO COOK EGGS

Eggs provide a potent blend of saturated fat, monounsaturated fat, and a small amount of polyunsaturated and omega-3 fatty acid. **Plus, they are an affordable, quick and easy meal.** There are numerous ways to prepare eggs. Some are better than others at preserving nutrients, but all of them are good. You can even use the microwave! But overall, shorter and lower-heat cooking methods cause less oxidation of cholesterol and help retain most of the nutrients in the eggs. **Whichever method you choose, be sure not to overcook them.**

DIFFERENT WAYS TO COOK EGGS

Hard Boiled Eggs

Hard-boiled eggs are cooked in their shells in a pot of boiling water for **6–10 minutes,** depending on how well cooked you want the yolk to be. The longer you cook them, the firmer the yolk will become. Hard-boiling protects the cholesterol in the yokes from oxidation. Oxidized cholesterol can result in potentially harmful compounds called oxysterols, which have been linked to heart disease. But nearly all dietary oxysterols come from fried junk food, not eggs.

When compared to baking eggs, hardboiled eggs lose only 18% of their vitamin D, whereas baking eggs can reduce vitamin D by 61%.

Poached Eggs

If your goal is to get the maximum nutrients out of your eggs, poaching them is the way to go. Poaching exposes eggs to relatively low heat for just a short period of time and leaves yokes intact.

Poach your eggs by simmering water between 160–180°F (71–82°C). Get the water spinning, then crack in an egg and let cook for 1–3 minutes.

Omelets

Be sure to keep the heat low to medium when cooking an omelet. Whisk the eggs and pour into a non-stick pan until they set. Top with leftover chopped ribeye or crumbled bacon if desired.

Scrambled

Scrambled eggs are beaten in a bowl, poured into a hot pan, and stirred over low heat until they set. **Feel free to add a tablespoon of heavy cream to the bowl for extra fat and more tender eggs.** Be sure to cook your eggs low and slow for a creamier finished product. A non-stick frying pan and a little bit of ghee are must-haves.

Though scrambling eggs exposes the cholesterol to heat and potential oxidation, it's not really something to worry about. If you are concerned, take the pan off the eat as soon as the eggs just set for a soft scramble.

Fried Eggs

Fried eggs are cooked on a skillet or non-stick pan and can be made with a runny yolk or cooked all the way through. **Use duck fat or ghee for extra fat and flavor,** but watch your heat! Fried eggs are delicious, but this cooking method uses high heat and may reduce the nutrients like cholesterol and vitamin A in the yolk if the pan is too hot.

Baked Eggs

Drop a couple of eggs into a lightly greased muffin pan or ramekin. You can sprinkle with a little grated cheese or ground beef, crumbled bacon or sausage for extra flavor. Cook at 375-degrees for 12-15 minutes depending on whether you prefer a hard yolk or runny yolk.

Chapter Seven

BENEFITS OF BUTTER

Butter is a mainstay of the BEBBIS Diet because it's fat in its purest, most natural form and a flavor-enhancer for any meat or protein. Butter is the most saturated of all the animal fats and a fantastic source of highly beneficial fatty acids like butyrate and Conjugate Linoleic Acid (CLA) that reduce inflammation and protect your heart.

Butter can help you meet the necessary fat-to-protein ratios that keep keto-carnivore sustainable. The healthy fats and nutrients in butter support heart and gut health while reducing the risk of various cancers.

Butter is also jam-packed with vitamins. Just two tablespoons (28 grams) of butter supplies 22% of your RDV of vitamin A (Retinol), which helps regulate hormone and thyroid function. It's an excellent source of Conjugated Linoleic Acid (CLA), which protects against heart disease and cancer, strengthens the immune system by reducing inflammation, and has anti-obesity properties. High concentrations of Butyrate, a gut-boosting fatty acid, support digestive health and may improve insulin sensitivity.

There are many kinds of butter available in grocery stores these days--salted, cultured, grass-fed, "European-style," ghee, whipped –the varieties seem endless. No matter what you choose to use, a cardinal rule is to avoid anything made with vegetable and seed oils. These products contain harmful plant antigens and phytochemicals that increase inflammation. **Margarine is a hard NO,** as are sunflower spreads and anything else made with plant "fats". Even certain spreads "made with olive oil" can be deceiving as they contain very little olive oil and mostly vegetable, canola, or safflower oil.

Raw Butter

Clarified Butter

WHICH BUTTER IS BETTER?

Pasture-Raised Grass-fed Butter

Grass-fed butter is obtained from the cows that feed exclusively on organic grass (as opposed to corn) and openly graze on vast pastures. Their diet doesn't contain any hormones or artificially processed food. The grass has higher levels of short-chain fatty acids, vitamin K2, and omega-3s. Therefore, grass-fed butter is the healthiest butter because it doesn't have any additives and is all natural.

- Grass-fed butter has been found to contain 26% more anti-inflammatory omega-3 fatty acids
- And it provides up to 500% more conjugated linoleic acid than butter from grain-fed cattle.
- Researchers believe grass-fed butter is much higher in vitamin K2 and the antioxidant beta-carotene.

This butter has additional benefits of omega-3 fatty acids and fat-soluble vitamins. Its taste is creamy and rich, and the color is bright yellow.

Raw Milk Butter

Raw milk butter is exactly as its name suggests... made from raw whole milk that has never been heated, processed, or otherwise altered in any fashion. Because raw butter has never been heated, it naturally possesses an abundance of bioavailable bacteria that aid in digestion. Researcher Rosalind Wulzen discovered that butter made from raw milk contained compounds that reduced stiffness and provided a number of dramatic benefits, including.

- Protection from calcification of the joints
- Protection from hardening of arteries
- Protection from cataracts
- Protection from calcification of the pineal gland

This butter has additional benefits of omega-3 fatty acids and fat-soluble vitamins. Its taste is creamy and rich, and the color is bright yellow.

Clarified Butter/Ghee

Clarified butter (also called ghee) is a good option for people who don't tolerate dairy well. In India, ghee is a sacred food and plays a role in many traditional medicines. Clarified butter is produced by heating butter or cream until it melts, then straining out the milk solids. During heating, the extra water evaporates. The result is pure butterfat that is saffron yellow in color with a rich consistency and nutty flavor that's great for high-heat cooking. Studies on animals show that ghee can lower cholesterol and triglycerides.

Though saturated animal fat has been maligned as public health threat since the 1960s, modern studies are proving butter and other animal fats to be nutrient-dense and packed with far more health benefits than previously believed.

The healthy fats, vitamins, and minerals work synergistically to support and enhance numerous physical functions, including immune health, fat metabolism, a healthy microbiome, intestinal integrity, and protection against type 2 diabetes and obesity.

Butter is highly satiating, loaded with nourishing fatty acids, and a good source of assorted vitamins. Lard, tallow, and duck fat are other good butter substitutes.

GRASS-FED BUTTER BENEFITS

Great Source of Butyrate

Great source of butyrate (a short-chain fatty acid) which reduces inflammation

Contains CLA

Contains CLA Conjugated Linoleic acid which helps reduce belly fat, helps to protect against cancer and supports muscle growth

Great Source of Vitamin D & K2

Great source of Vitamin K2- may reverse arterial calcification and helps not increase bone density

Contains Vitamin A- Retinol

Contains Vitamin A- which is good for the thyroid, adrenals, and cardiovascular health

Additional Beneficial Nutrients

-Lecithin
-Selenium
-Magnesium
-Zinc
-Copper
-Iodine
...and more!

Contains Essential Fat

Butter is rich in Omega 3 Fatty Acids that reduce inflammation and improve hormone optimization.

AFFIRMATIONS

All I need is within me

I love the person I am becoming

With more practice, it will get easier

I can get through anything

POSITIVE MINDSET

I am brave and resilient

You are your only limit

I'm still learning, I'll keep trying!

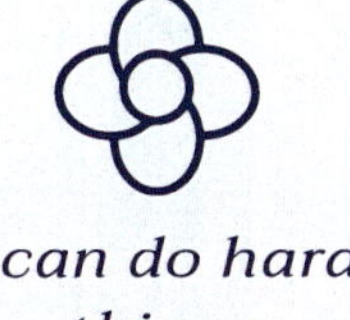

I can do hard things

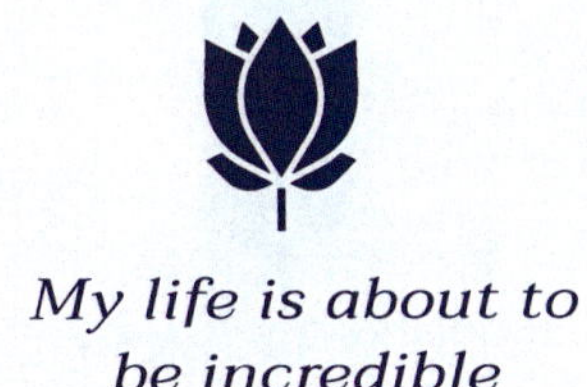

My life is about to be incredible

I am stronger than I know

Chapter Eight

IMPORTANCE OF SALT

Salt is an Electrolyte

Salt is classified as an electrolyte. In the nutrition world, "electrolyte" refers to minerals that create electrically charged ions when dissolved in the body's fluids.

Different electrolytes often work together to accomplish important tasks. For instance, sodium and potassium help conduct the electricity critical for nerve impulses and contraction of muscles. These two electrolytes also maintain the correct balance of fluids inside and outside of your cells, keeping them from shriveling up or exploding. Salt and other electrolytes also keep us hydrated, and balance our blood pH so it doesn't become too acidic.

The terms salt and sodium are often used interchangeably, but they're not the same thing. **Salt is food, while sodium is a mineral present in many foods, including meat, yogurt and vegetables.** The salt/sodium confusion exists because salt is the richest source of sodium in our diets. Studies have found that 70% of the average person's sodium intake comes from the salt in processed foods. **Baking soda and foods that rely on it (baked goods, breads, cookies) also contain sodium.**

Why we need Salt

Both humans and animals naturally crave salt. That's because the sodium and chloride found in salt are essential minerals. In nutrition, the word "essential" means that our bodies can't make it on their own. Adequate salt intake has been shown to:

- **Maintain delicate fluid balances within and around cells**
- **Maintain a healthy blood pressure**
- **Help muscles contract efficiently**
- **Help nerves send their signals**

Salt is so critical to neurotransmission — the sending of signals from neuron to neuron — that low salt intake can increase seizures in those with epilepsy. Though sodium levels are regulated by various organs and hormones, not consuming enough salt can trigger a stress response as the body tries to avoid a condition called hyponatremia.

While eating BEBBIS, salt is a critical component. Your body uses salt to help regulate fluid balance. As you're eating fewer processed foods and your body begins to sheds electrolytes and fluids while in ketosis, your body also loses salt. Even transitioning from regular keto to B.E.B.B.I.S., you will lose extra water from inflammation.

How do you know you need more salt? Feeling foggy (brain fog) or lethargic, muscle cramps/spasms, headache/dehydration/hungover, dizziness going from sitting to standing are all likely symptoms.

The solution is usually more salt. If you add a little more sea salt to your diet and you feel better, then that's your answer. Often salting your food to taste isn't enough to compensate for the volume of salt you've lost. When more salt doesn't do the trick, you may need to try adding potassium or magnesium. Soaking in an Epsom Salt bath can also help as you absorb salt's active ingredients magnesium and sulfate through your skin.

Like red meat, salt has been demonized, but that other white crystalline substance (sugar) is a much bigger threat than salt ever was! New studies are showing that salt may not be as damaging to health as previously claimed. There's growing evidence to suggest that a moderate intake of sodium may have a beneficial role in cardiovascular health, but a potentially more harmful role when intake is very high or very low.

For those who want to go dairy-free, but have difficulty kicking the dairy habit, salt is sometimes one of the problems. There are lots of salty cheeses. If your body is craving salt, it can make removing dairy products more challenging.

TYPES OF SALT

There are many types of salt. Every part of the world has its own primary source of salt, and each source has its own look, taste, and characteristics

Table Salt

Also known as rock salt, table salt is the most popular form of salt in many countries. It's mined from underground areas that were once ancient seas. Table salt can be used to cure meat, fish, and other animal products. **It's usually fortified with iodine, a pro-thyroid element.**

Himalayan Salt

Himalayan salt is a special type of rock salt. It comes from salt caves located deep in the Himalayas. This type of salt is known for its trace mineral content, which gives it a pink-hued color. Himalayan salt is also popular among health-conscious people.

Sea Salt

Sea salt has quickly become popular among health-conscious types. It comes from present-day seawater, from which it's harvested through evaporation. **Sea salt is coarser, flakier, and more flavorful than regular table salt.** As an added plus, it often contains small amounts of naturally-occurring iodine.

Kosher Salt

Kosher salt is basically table salt without the added iodine. It's used by many ethnic groups, especially the Jewish, for dehydrating and preserving meat. **Kosher salt may contain fewer impurities than other types of salt,** though some varieties contain anti-caking agents. Its delightful taste makes kosher salt popular among chefs.

Recommended Salts

Himalayan Pink Salt	Redmond Real Salt	Maldon Sea Salt Flakes	Other high-quality natural sea or colored salts

Chapter Nine

CARNIVORE FOR BABIES

From breast to bone

The carnivore diet provides all the nutrients your growing children need from the time they are breastfeeding as a baby to when they are toddlers and young adults.

There is no risk of malnutrition if the carnivore diet is done properly. Children will get every nutrient that their growing bodies need from calcium, vitamin C, vitamin A, and vitamin K to folate.

There is no conclusive evidence that a diet high in meat causes cancer, heart disease and numerous other health problems that you might have been warned about by your doctors.

From an evolutionary perspective, if this diet had been unsafe, our ancestors wouldn't have survived. The fact that they not only survived but thrived on a heavily meat-based diet tells us otherwise.

In The Womb

Staying carnivore throughout pregnancy is ideal, but many women struggle to do so. Meat aversions and nausea are fairly common in the first and second trimester, even in women with a long history of carnivore eating.

About 80% of pregnant women experience food aversions and nausea. Ultimately, you have to listen to your body and return to carnivore as tolerated.

On the Breast

Breast feeding is an extremely efficient process, which is great for babies but can be less advantageous for mothers. The body not only prioritizes nutrient intake for breastmilk but can steal from the mother's stores, even taking calcium from the mother's bones if necessary. Even under starvation conditions, the body still produces breastmilk with a remarkably nutrient dense profile.

As comforting and amazing as this might be, it's important for mothers to nourish their own bodies. Research suggests that breastmilk displays a remarkably stable nutrient profile regardless of the mother's food intake. Nonetheless, some nutrient levels are more dependent upon dietary intake because the body doesn't store them in any substantial volume. Over time, deficiencies can develop. Optimal nutrition is crucial both for the baby's development and the nursing mother's overall health. **Meat-based eating is a great way to ensure nutrient**

To support breast feeding, the more nutrient dense a nursing mother's diet is, the better. Nursing moms require an additional 500-700 calories for breastmilk production. But specific nutrient needs rise during nursing. With only the basic RDA intake, women may lose substantial bone, muscle and other organ stores.

The most common deficiencies for nursing women are zinc and calcium. Other "at risk" nutrients include magnesium, thiamine, vitamin E, vitamin D, B6, and iron. Nutrients like folate are also a concern because the body keeps no ready stores and excretes any excess. It's important to realize that absorption efficiencies vary nutrient by nutrient. Without plant antigens and antinutrients to block absorption, a meat-based diet helps ensure maximum vitamin and mineral intake.

At the Table

As consumers of breast milk for all of their nutritional needs, **babies are natural carnivores from birth.** To give your child the best possible start in life, avoid as much processed food as possible. Choosing nutritionally-dense meats and animal products is an easy way to do this. **Children can thrive on an animal-based diet from the time they wean and begin eating solid foods.** Decades-old research by Chicago pediatrician Clara M. Davis showed that when given access to only nutrient-dense foods, **young children will choose what they need for optimal growth and development.**

Young toddlers are instinctual, and if they are in a **'healthy food bubble'** where they have never tasted sugar or refined carbohydrates, they most likely will choose exactly what their bodies need. Nutrients on the carnivore diet come in highly bioavailable forms and are free from plant toxins.

When they start on solid food, make meat and organ meat (especially those from ruminants) the center of their diets and occasionally let them have some seasonal fruits and vegetables if they enjoy. **Fresh, whole food is the key.** A bit of seasonal plant food, if they have no problem with it, should be fine.

Children are very smart; if you let them choose, they'll likely go for meat and some fruits but probably won't touch vegetables, especially the plain, unprocessed ones. And if you feed them fresh whole fruits, you don't need to worry about the amount of carbs in there, it's hard to eat a lot of fresh whole fruits. **And it's important to limit grains, seed oils, and all processed foods if you can.**

Easy-to-eat Carnivore finger foods include:

- Hamburger or Salmon patties
- Meatballs
- Scrambled or chopped hard-boiled eggs
- Chicken or beef stock or bone broth in a cup
- Chicken thighs with the skin on
- Beef ribs

By setting a good example, being consistent, and explaining to them the reasoning behind your food choices, your children will begin to understand and appreciate why animal-based eating is a smart choice.

Chapter Ten

BEBBIS SUCCESS STORIES

Bianca & Travis's Story

My husband Travis and I tried to grow our family for seven years with two years of IVF treatments. It has been nothing short of a tiresome and heartbreaking process as it is for many families struggling with infertility.

My husband and I first started with assisted reproductive treatments (ART) in 2016. After a few years without any success, we sought medical advice. I was placed on Clomid, and after three rounds, I suffered my first chemical pregnancy.

In 2017 we attended a local fertility clinic, and after we made it through all of the preliminary tests I was diagnosed with "unexplained infertility." We became financially strained due to my insurance declining any further coverage, and we were unable to continue with any ART treatments.

Devastated, we continued to try naturally without any success for the next three years. In 2020 we were able to return to the local fertility clinic and underwent three rounds of IUI without any success.

I was at a loss and was giving up hope until one day a friend of mine introduced me to one of her friends who found success with IVF at CNY. She told me all about CNY fertility and sold me on scheduling a consultation.

From the first consultation and every interaction after, I was very pleased with the knowledge, kindness, and understanding of all of the medical staff.

We were able to afford the cost of IVF and were so grateful. We underwent retrieval and a fresh transfe which failed Further testing via ReceptivaDx revealed signs of endometriosis and low AMH.

I was treated with two months of Lupron Depot before my FET on 10/05/2021. Unfortunately, our cycle failed. After two failed rounds of IVF, my husband and I were devastated. Upon a follow-up consultation with a CNY Provider and consultation with my OBGYN, laparoscopy was recommended as a treatment for my endometriosis.

The surgery took place on December 9, 2021, which resulted in the removal of one of my Fallopian tubes, which was blocked, and a diagnosis of stage 3 endometriosis.

We went back to CNY Colorado for a third round in hopes of bringing home our miracle. Unfortunately, that failed too with two beautiful 5 Day embryos. After this, our Church and our community helped raise funds to help us make it to Syracuse and try again.

We underwent a third round of IVF and our 4th transfer, which yielded only one embryo and resulted in a failed transfer. The following month we returned for a FET cycle, and our 5th transfer failed yet again leaving us devastated. But we were determined and willing to fight through this to bring home our baby.

We sold the motorcycle and, eventually, our home to afford further treatment. Immunology testing took place next, and we discovered that I had elevated NKC (Natural Killer Cells) and a possible APS diagnosis.

Eventually, we reached out directly to Dr. Kiltz and he recommended we both transition to a carnivore (low inflammation) lifestyle and diet.

I credit the transition as the "missing link" to receiving our little miracle. Along with the transition to Carnivore, I was also placed on an immune protocol that would also help to suppress the immune system enough to accept an embryo.

After just 74 days of following a strict Carnivore lifestyle, I experienced the following results: depression disappeared, painful periods were a thing of the past, bloating disappeared, my hair grew back, cystic acne disappeared, psoriasis cleared up, and I felt stronger and able to lift heavier in the gym.

My husband and I returned to CNY Syracuse for a 6th transfer of two Day 5 embryos. We shared a prayer with the CNY staff after the transfer was complete. For the first time during this entire two-year IVF process, I felt peace and confidence after the transfer because I knew we had done all we possibly could.

At the time of beta testing, nine short days later, I tested positive for pregnancy! Our beautiful little girl was born on Easter Sunday, 2023. God is Good.

Hope, Inspiration & Advice:

I wish I would have known about Dr. Kiltz and the carnivore lifestyle sooner!

The many benefits I have received are the reason why I have continued with an animal-based diet and approach throughout my pregnancy, into my breastfeeding journey and to today. I will continue this way of eating for the rest of my life.

Photo credit: @Saraannphoto

Nina & Charlie's Story

My husband and I had been trying to have a baby since we married in 2014. Before we found CNY, we had 6 unsuccessful IUI's done by other doctors in Maryland. When they weren't changing any of their protocol, we began to wonder if there was something else out there. Not to mention they denied my IVF cycle due to my BMI. Being a plus-sized woman battling infertility is a very hard place to be. I've had doctors tell me I should just give up and adopt.

Fast forward to me joining some IVF groups on social media and finding Tanya, an angel on earth. **She told me about CNY and their judgment-free zone and supportive staff. I thought it was too good to be true.** But I put my faith in them and made an appointment.

We went to Albany for our very first retrieval in August of 2018. Everyone was so amazing. They never made me feel like a plus-size woman. They didn't label me. They just made me feel welcome. They were out of this world!

In 2018, we continued to do three more retrievals and did five FETs. We were so hopeful when a couple of them took, but sadly all ended in early miscarriages.

We decided to go to Syracuse next. We met with Dr. Corley and Dr. Kiltz. I was star-struck. You will come to find that these are the most humble, down-to-earth men there are. They are truly here to help you in any way they can. We did two more retrievals and ended up with five embryos! We thought for sure it was going to work. But again, it didn't.

I felt like a failure. I felt like my body was failing to do what it was meant to do! I had a phone call with Dr. Kiltz where I cried my eyes out and told him I felt like this was never going to happen for us. He assured me that was not the case.

Dr. Kiltz changed my protocol to basically kill my immune system (I have an autoimmune disease). **He told me I should try Keto to eliminate the inflammation associated with my endometriosis.** I took vitamins and the medications that he recommended. I planned to do this for three months, and then to do another FET.

But...we had a surprise coming that we couldn't believe with our own eyes! I was PREGNANT!!!!

I think I bought out the local Walgreens of pregnancy tests because there was no way this could happen. After seven years?? No way. But it was true. With Dr. Kiltz's direction, I had a miracle growing inside me.

My pregnancy was wonderful, easy, and without complication. I gave birth to our beautiful son on December 12, 2021. He's our everything.

Due to complications with my endometriosis, after I had my son, I knew I would need a hysterectomy. It wasn't life-threatening, but it would dramatically improve my quality of life.

Now the thing is, we still have four sweet embryos frozen at CNY. People say, "Why does it matter? You already have a baby! You should be grateful!" And boy, are we. But we would love a sibling for our son.

So here we are! Back at it. We are starting our journey once again. We're excited, nervous, and hopeful! We plan to do a FET in the upcoming months. We must lift each other during these hard times and keep the faith that our miracles will happen! **If anyone can make our dreams a reality, it's CNY!**

Photo credit: Connor Lange

Emily and Jesse's Story

Before this journey, we never imagined that infertility Jesse and I were married in October 2017 and knew we wanted to start a family right away. We began trying by tracking ovulation but were disappointed each month with negative pregnancy tests. My cycles were pretty normal, maybe a little longer here and there, but nothing that stood out to me as super concerning.

By Spring 2019, after a year and a half, I mentioned to my local NP that we were really struggling. We talked about Ovulation Induction and started with blood work, an ultrasound, HSG and semen analysis. Everything came back normal, which made things even more frustrating as to why we weren't getting pregnant.

In Fall of 2019, we started our first round of Ovulation Induction. We did a round of Clomid, a trigger shot, and timed intercourse with no luck. My second cycle, I asked to switch to Letrozole (I had a close friend who took one round of Letrozole and got pregnant on the first try). My body was pretty unresponsive to the Letrozole; my follicles barely grew.

After 4 back-to-back unsuccessful cycles, my husband and I decided we needed abreak. Infertility really weighed on me, I felt less like myself than I ever had, and knowing that all my testing was "normal" made things even more frustrating and difficult to understand.

In the fall, we came to the decision that we needed to give ourselves the best chance possible at a successful pregnancy. **After tons of research, my husband and I found CNY Fertility.**

I took my infertility into my own hands and we started doing everything we could that would help us in building a family. I started the KETO diet. My husband and I started taking the supplements that were recommended on the CNY website, and I did something I never thought I would do, acupuncture (which I ended up loving!).

In March 2021, I had our phone consult with a CNY NP. She was super informative and I was told that my AMH was pretty high, giving me the diagnosis of PCOS. We decided on jumping right into IVF since our previous treatments were so unsuccessful, and I didn't want to do something that I already knew hadn't worked.

I had my first egg retrieval May 1, 2021. I had 26 eggs removed, and I felt like everything was finally looking up for the first time in a long time. Unfortunately, only one embryo survived. We transferred our little embryo on May 31, 2021 with Dr. Corley.Dr. Corley was so great, he was calm, and made me feel so relaxed and hopeful. He prayed over us once our embryo was transferred. Sadly, our little embryo did not stick and we were devastated. I felt like we had done everything we could and felt very defeated. But we weren't giving up.

I scheduled a follow-up appointment and decided to repeat an HSG with Dr. Kiltz just to see if anything had changed from my first one. It was unremarkable, which was good news. He talked with me about continuing Keto, changing up my medications for our next round of IVF, and suggested I take the next cycle to prime. I was so grateful to be able to get his recommendations. I started priming with HGH, estrogen and progesterone right away.

In August 2021, we were ready to start our next round of IVF. I started stimming with a new regimen and I was so excited. I had 32 eggs retrieved this time!

After a few days, I found out that we had 11 frozen embryos! We transferred our best-graded embryo on September 13, 2022. I was lucky enough to have Dr. Corley perform our transfer again.

On September 22, 2022 the CNY nurse called with my results and I was PREGNANT!

I was so excited and shocked; I honestly don't remember much of the phone call. I took my first-ever positive pregnancy test as soon as I got off the phone with her. **The word "pregnant" came up on the screen, and I cried so many tears of happiness.**

I wrapped it up as a gift for my husband, went out and bought a baby outfit and book, and surprised him when he got home, something I had waited so long to be able to do!

We kept the gender of baby and the names we had picked out a surprise until the arrival. Our miracle baby boy, Emmett, arrived June 5, 2022 and is now a happy and healthy 7-month old!

Helpful resources Emily & Jesse found:

Personally, support was EVERYTHING. I was not super open about my infertility, let alone that my husband and I were going through IVF. Very, very, few people knew.

However, the people that did know were always there for us. My husband really let me take the reins on everything and supported and trusted my decision making in growing our family.

He ate any meal I made following the KETO diet, no matter how weird it might've been. My best friend followed the KETO diet with me and we exercised daily, keeping each other accountable. She helped and supported us in more ways than I could ever explain.

Chapter Eleven

SAUCES & SNACKS RECIPES

BLUE CHEESE BUTTER

A rich and flavorful topping for meat recipes with very little prep. Easy to make ahead and store for up to a month.

Ingredients

 2 TBSP Butter

 2 TBSP Blue Cheese

METHOD
Stove top melt

TOTAL TIME
5 Minutes

SERVINGS
1-2

Instructions

- Place 2 TBSP of Butter and 2 TBSP of Blue Cheese (or any amount you plan on eating or would like to have stored in your fridge - stores perfectly for up to one week in air tight container in the fridge) in a stainless steel measuring cup and place on the burner to melt, stirring occasionally.
- **Notes:** If you don't have a stainless steel measuring cup, simply melt the butter and cheese together using a method of your choosing.
- You don't have to do a 50/50 mix. Everyone will have different taste preferences, so experiment. 50/50 is a good starting place but then try 25% butter 75% blue cheese, then 75% butter, 25% blue cheese, etc. You don't even need a measuring spoon, I can't remember the last time I actually used one.

BROWN BUTTER

WIth its unmistakable nutty aroma, brown butter is also known as "liquid gold." It takes mere minutes to make and is an easy way to boost flavor. Enjoy as a drizzle over meat or fish.

Ingredients

 1 Stick of Butter

METHOD
Stove top melt

TOTAL TIME
5- 10 Minutes

SERVINGS
2-20

Instructions

- Place one stick of butter in a pot or saucepan on medium heat stirring lightly for about 5 minutes.
- Once the butter begins to foam or light golden flakes, begin to appear start stirring vigorously. After about 10-30 seconds (depending upon the cooking temperature and how "browned" you want your butter) a substantial number of golden flakes will have appeared. Remove from heat and transfer to a cool dish or container and let cool for at least a few minutes.
- Can be enjoyed immediately or stored in an airtight container in the fridge for at least one week and remelted any time you want to use.

EASY HOLLANDAISE SAUCE

A rich and creamy sauce with a little tang made with BEBBIS staples. Quick and easy to make with a blender or immersion blender.

Ingredients

 1/2 cup of grass-fed butter

 3 free-range egg yolks

 Redmond Real Sea Salt to taste

 1 1/2 tablespoons of raw apple cider vinegar

METHOD
Stove top melt

TOTAL TIME
5- 10 Minutes

SERVINGS
2-20

Instructions

- Separate your eggs saving just the yolks and place them in your blender (if using) or bowl. You can save the whites for something else.
- Melt butter in a saucepan over low heat and allow to cool slightly
- Add vinegar to bowl or blender.
- Slowly blend the yolk/vinegar mixture on lowest speed and gradually add melted butter in a steady stream.
- Add sea salt to taste.
- Serve warm or chilled on eggs, meats, fish, or anything that could use a tasty sauce.

CARNIVORE MAYO

Perfect for adding flavor and creaminess to your low-carb, carnivore meals.

Ingredients

 2 Egg Yolks

 1 TBSP Apple Cider Vinegar

 1 cup bacon or duck fat - *liquid but not hot or it will cook eggs"*

 1/2 teaspoon sea salt

METHOD
Stove top melt

TOTAL TIME
6- 10 Minutes

SERVINGS
1-2

Instructions

- Cool a skinny container like a wide-mouth mason jar that has just enough room for an immersion blender to fit in the freezer for about 10 minutes.
- Place the egg yolks, followed by vinegar, and finally, the bacon fat and salt in the mason jar.
- Place an immersion blender at the bottom of the jar and turn the blender on. Move the immersion blender up at an extremely slow pace, so that it takes approximately 1 minute to get to the top. This should emulsify all of the ingredients. Continue to pulsate the blender up and down quickly until desired creaminess is achieved.
- Can be stored in the refridgerator for approximately 1 week.

HOMEMADE SOUR CREAM

Sour cream is equal parts fun and yum as a carnivore diet condiment. Make your own homemade sour cream with heavy cream and cultured buttermilk.

Ingredients

-  Heavy Cream
-  Cultured Buttermilk

METHOD
Stove top melt

TOTAL TIME
5- 10 Minutes

SERVINGS
1-2

Instructions

- Simply mix the two ingredients in a jar, tightly screw on a lid and store in the dark at room temperature for 24 hours.

CARNIVORE CHEESE SAUCE

Carnivore cheese sauce is a velvety, salty, satiating condiment with major nutrional benefits.

Ingredients

 3 oz. soft cheese like camembert or creamy blue cheese

 1/3 cup of heavy cream

 3 tablespoons of butter

 1 cup shredded cheddar cheese

 1/2 teaspoon of kosher salt

METHOD
Stove top melt

TOTAL TIME
6- 10 Minutes

SERVINGS
1-2

Instructions

- Put the cream and butter into a saucepan and gently heat.
- Add the grated cheddar cheese and soft creamy cheese.
- Stir until melted and bring to a simmer.
- Remove from heat once it begins to bubble.
- Mix until smooth and creamy.
- For a thicker sauce, cook for 3-5 more minutes while stirring.
- If it gets too thick, add a splash of water or cream.

TWISTED BACON SNACK STICKS

A delicious and portable carnivore snack stick.

Ingredients

 1/2 lb Bacon

METHOD

Stove top melt

TOTAL TIME

6- 10 Minutes

SERVINGS

1-2

Instructions

- Take a single piece of bacon and twist it in an upwards motion so it resembles a straight line (not wrapped around itself like a piece of sushi). Then, line them up side-by-side on a parchment-lined baking sheet.
- Bake them in a 350° oven for around 20 minutes. Flip the twists and bake for another 20 minutes. You're left with perfect twists of bacon that are great for breakfast and to-go snacks. This is also an incredibly efficient way to cook a lot of bacon if you're meal-prepping for the week.

THE BENEFITS OF BONE BROTH

A warm and comforting recipe for any time of the year, Carnivore Bone Broth is a delicious treat that can be used as:

 A warm drink

 To braise meat

 Add it to carnivore stews or soups

Bone broth is nutrient-dense, can help with inflammation and contains significant amounts
of essential amino acids, collagen, and gelatin.

It also may help with:

 Weight management

 Better hydration

 Improved sleep

 Reduced joint pain

Minimizing inflammation

Drinking bone broth is an excellent way to break your fast and to quickly boost electrolyte levels. In traditional fasting, many carnivores only drink water with a pinch of salt. Other carnivores swear by bone broth while fasting.

What bones are best and where to get them?

When making bone broth, your butcher really is your best friend. Ask a deal on a combination of different bones as that makes for the best broth. Beef, lamb, mutton, goat, pork and/or the bones of any other ruminant animal can be used to make carnivore bone broth.

Ideally, you want a mix of meaty bones, marrow bones, joint bones and knuckle bones. Oxtail also works great. Simmering a diverse array of bone types ensures you get broth from marrow, cartilage, sinew, and connective tissue.

Breaking Down the Bones:

Many bone broth recipes call for the use of apple cider vinegar, lime and/or lemon juice. All of these mediums are acidic and may help to break down the bones extracting more vitamins and minerals.

YOU DO NOT NEED TO USE ANY SORT OF ACID TO BREAK DOWN BONES!

Cooking low and slow will ensure you get all the vitamins and minerals you need.

Don't Be Afraid to Add Some Meat:

If you're looking to add some additional protein to your broth, add meaty bones or collagen rich meat.

Any meat you add will come out slow-cooked and delicious. Ask your butcher for beef cheeks, shanks, or any other meaty bone/ tough cut of meat.

BONE BROTH

Restorative and nourishing, Bone Broth is a savory, nutrient-dense, and collagen-rich liquid made from simmering marrow-rich animal bones (beef, chicken, turkey, pork) in water for an extended period of time.

Ingredients

Lots of bone, Variety is good (marrow, knuckle, etc), however many you want.
Let's try starting with 5-10 lbs

Water

Optional: 2 TBSP apple or white vinegar

METHOD
Stove top

TOTAL TIME
6- 10 Minutes

SERVINGS
1-2

Instructions

- **Optional: Roasting Bones** –Place bones in a single layer on a large roasting tray and place them in the oven at 450°F (232°C) for about 20 minutes, until golden brown. Remove bones from the oven and place bones in a large stockpot.
- **Optional:** Fill the Stockpot with water and vinegar bring to a boil, skimming the foam and other floaties that come to the top for about 5 minutes. Dump the water out and rinse any remaining foam off the bones.
- **Required Step -** Traditional: Fill the stockpot up with water bones in a large stockpot until the bones are fully covered. Bring water to a boil, then reduce to the lowest of simmers and cover for 24 hours.
- **Required Step - Alternative/Pressure Cooker:** If you have a pressure cooker and don't have 24 hours, a pressure cooker is a great alternative to getting all the amazing nutrients out of bones in a short amount of time.
- Add bones and enough water to cover the bones in the pressure cooker. Close and lock the lid. Follow manufacturers instruction and cook for 120-180 minutes.
- Release pressure using the natural-release method according to manufacturer's instructions, 10 to 40 minutes. Unlock and remove the lid. Remove bones and discard.
- Cool and enjoy.

Chapter Twelve

BEEF RECIPES

REVERSE SEARED STEAK

Slow-cooked in the oven, then finished with a hot sear. Steak cooked this way turns out pink from edge to edge with a beautiful exterior crust.

Ingredients

-  1 lbs thick (at least 1.5 inches) fatty well marbled, flavorful cut of beef (ribeye, NY Strip, etc).
-  Kosher, Sea, or Pink Salt
-  Optional: 1 TBSP Tallow

METHOD

Oven Broiled

TOTAL TIME

6- 10 Minutes

SERVINGS

1-2

Instructions

- Put the steak on a wire rack in a baking sheet with a digital meat thermometer set to alarm when the steak is 20 degrees below your desired doneness. Set oven to somewhere between 200 and 250°F; you can put the steak in the oven immediately or wait for it to come to temperature - I would just put it in.
- As the steak reach approximately 25-30 degrees below your final desired temp, heat a heavy pan on high on the stovetop. When the steak reaches 20 degrees below the desired doneness and the alarm sounds, remove the steak from the oven. Put 1-2 TBSP of tallow in the now ripping hot pan. Add the steak and frequently flip with tongs until a beautiful crust has formed. Ensure the steak is removed from the pan before it reaches 10-15 degrees below your final desired doneness.
- Let the steak rest on a wire rack, cutting board, or plate until the desired doneness is reached through carryover cooking. Slice, top with salt to taste, and dip in brown or blue cheese butter. Celebrate.

PAN SEARED STEAK

No grill? No problem. Pan-seared steak comes out juicy, tender, and flavorful. Let it rest before slicing so it has time to reabsorb juices.

Ingredients

 1 lbs thick (at least 1.5 inches) fatty well marbled, flavorful cut of beef (ribeye, NY Strip, etc).

 Kosher, Sea, or Pink Salt

 1 TBSP Tallow

 2 TBSP Butter

 2 TBSP Blue Cheese

METHOD
Pan Seared

TOTAL TIME
10 Minutes

SERVINGS
1-2

Instructions

- Salt the steak liberally a minimum of 45 minutes before cooking. Ideally, salt the steak and keep it on a wire rack in the fridge for 4-48 hours before cooking. If you don't have 45 minutes salt either immediately before or wait until after the steak is cooked to salt.
- Using a heavy-bottomed pan (cast iron or stainless steel), preheat the pan with 1 TBSP Tallow.
- Pat dry with a clean towel to pull away any moisture. This will improve the browning Maillard reaction which creates a great crust and flavor.
- Once the tallow begins to smoke, carefully place the steak inside the pan, pushing down slightly to ensure contact with the pan throughout the full steak.
- frequently flip with tongs until browned on all sides including the edges until it reaches 15-20 degrees below your desired temperature, usually 6 to 12 minutes depending on thickness and preferred doneness of the steak. The steak will continue to cook once removed from the pan.
- Sprinkle with Flaky Salt immediately after taking the steak off the pan (the amount of salt should be to taste and depend on how much you put on before cooking)
- Let the steak rest on a wire rack, plate or cutting board for 5-10 minutes - until the steak reaches desired doneness.
- While steak is resting (or while cooking) place 2 TBSP of Butter and 2 TBSP of Blue Cheese in a stainless steel measuring cup and place on the burner to melt, stirring occasionally. If you don't have a stainless steel measuring cup, simply melt the butter and cheese together using a method of your choosing.

OVEN BROILED STEAK

Broiling steaks is a great option when it's too cold to grill outside, or you don't have time to fire up the grill. Best for steaks that are less than 1.5 inches thick.

Ingredients

1 lbs thick (at least 1.5 inches) fatty well marbled, flavorful cut of beef (ribeye, NY Strip, etc).

Kosher, Sea, or Pink Salt

Optional: 1 TBSP Tallow

METHOD

Pan Seared

TOTAL TIME

10 Minutes

SERVINGS

1-2

Instructions

- Move the oven rack 6 inches from the heating element.
- Preheat the oven and cast iron or stainless steel skillet by setting the oven to broil for 5 to 20 minutes. If desired, place a TBSP or two of butter, tallow, or ghee in the pan a minute or two before putting the steak into the oven.
- Once the skillet is preheated, pull out the oven rack and carefully lay pre-salted (refer to page ____ steaks) on the skillet. NOTE: Pan is Extremely Hot and will spit and splatter.
- Close the oven or leave it slightly ajar as you normally would when using the broader and sear the steaks for 3 minutes on one side, and turn and sear the opposite side for 3 minutes. DO NOT USE A FORK TO TURN STEAKS!
- Once the desired level of crust has formed, you can switch the oven to 500F and cook until your steak reaches 15-20 degrees below your desired level of doneness.
- Remove steak from oven and hot pan and hit with flaky salt immediately. Let sit on a wire rack, cutting board, or plate until carry-over cooking has brought your steak to your desired level of doneness, then slice.
- Optional: dip every bite in delicious blue cheese butter or browned butter.

SALISBURY STEAK

Topped with rich and savory meat juices, Salisbury Steak is a comfort food staple.

Ingredients

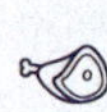 Your preferred size hamburger patty for each person eating. Try a 1/3 -1/2 lbs patty if you don't know where to start.

 1/2 cup meat juice from sous vide chuck roast (or beef broth)

 1 TBSP Red Wine Vinegar (optional)

 2-4 TBSP Butter

 1 tsp Grass fed beef collagen.

 Kosher, Sea, or Pink Salt

METHOD
Stove top

TOTAL TIME
30 Minutes

SERVINGS
1-2

Instructions

- Preheat a heavy bottom pan, ideally stainless steel, and press formed patties firmly into the pan. Cook until thoroughly browned, then flip and cook until fully cooked.
- Ideally in the same pan, pour meat juice or broth and allow to simmer while scraping any stuck-on browned bits (fond) so they become part of the sauce. Add red wine vinegar and cook for 1 minute. Add 2-4 TBSP of butter and stir continuously until butter is homogenously mixed into the sauce. Add gelatin and simmer until desired thickness is achieved.
- Pour sauce over cooked burger patty and enjoy.

GROUND BEEF FRITTATA

A delicious breakfast or lunch with rich, meaty flavor.

Ingredients

 4.5 oz / 125g ground beef

 3 eggs

 1 oz / 25g cream cheese

METHOD
Stove top

TOTAL TIME
30 Minutes

SERVINGS
1-2

Instructions

- Preheat oven to 350° F.
- Cook ground beef in a frying pan over medium heat
- Once cooked through, remove from heat and add cream cheese. Stir until melted and combined.
- Cool slightly, then pour beaten egg over the top and bake for 10-15 min. in oven until eggs are fully set.
- Slice in pie shaped portions and serve.

SOUS VIDE SMOKED BRISKET RECIPE

Sous vide (pronounced sue-veed) means "under vacuum" in French and refers to the process of vacuum-sealing food in a bag then cooking it to a very precise temperature in a water bath.

Ingredients

2 1/4 ounces kosher salt (about 1/4 cup; 65g)

1/4 ounce (10g) pink salt, such as Prague Powder Curing Salt (optional; see notes)

1 flat-cut or point-cut brisket, about 5 pounds (2.25kg); see notes

METHOD

Pan Seared

TOTAL TIME

Up to 78 hours

SERVINGS

1-2

Instructions

- Combine salt, and pink salt (if using) in a small bowl. Rub two-thirds of mixture evenly over surface of brisket. Reserve remaining one-third of mixture. Slice brisket in half crosswise in order to fit into large vacuum bags.
- Place each brisket half in a vacuum bag. (Fold over the top of each bag while you add brisket so that no rub or juices get on the edges of bags, which can weaken the seal.) Add 4 drops (about 1/8 teaspoon) liquid smoke, if using, to each bag. Seal bags using a vacuum sealer and let rest for 2 to 3 hours in the refrigerator.
- Set your precision cooker to 135°F (57°C) for brisket with a tender, steak-like texture.. Add brisket to water bath and cover it with a lid, aluminum foil. Cook for 24 to 36 hours at 155°F or 36 to 72 hours at 135°F. Allow cooked brisket to cool at least to room temperature before proceeding. Brisket can be stored in the refrigerator at this stage for up to 1 week before finishing.
- Pieces of vacuum-sealed brisket being placed into sous-vide machine.
- To Finish on the Grill: Light 1/2 chimney full of charcoal. When all charcoal is lit and covered with gray ash, pour out and arrange coals on one side of charcoal grate. Set cooking grate in place, cover grill, and allow to preheat for 5 minutes. Alternatively, set half the burners on a gas grill to medium-high heat, cover, and preheat for 10 minutes. Clean and oil grilling grate.
- Remove brisket from bags and carefully blot dry with paper towels. Rub re-served salt and pepper mixture into surface of brisket. Place brisket on cooler side of grill, fat cap up. Add 4 to 5 hardwood chunks to hotter side of grill. (If using a gas grill, wrap wood chunks loosely in aluminum foil before placing over hotter side of grill.) Cover and allow brisket to smoke, adjusting vents to maintain a temperature between 275 and 300°F (135 and 149°C) and adding 2 to 3 wood chunks twice during cooking. Smoke until a deep, dark bark has formed, about 3 hours. Continue with step 7.
- To Finish in the Oven: Adjust oven rack to lower-middle position and preheat oven to 300°F (150°C). (If your oven has a convection setting, turn it on and adjust heat to 275°F/135°C instead.) Remove brisket from sous vide bags and carefully blot dry with paper towels. (Liquid from bags can be added to your favorite barbecue sauce and simmered down to provide extra flavor.) Rub reserved salt-and-pepper mixture into surface of brisket. Place brisket on a wire rack set in a rimmed baking sheet, fat cap up, and place in oven. Roast until a deep, dark bark has formed, about 2 hours. Continue with step 7.
- Hunk of brisket with dark crust resting on wire rack over a baking sheet.
- Transfer brisket to a cutting board and tent with foil. Allow to rest until the temperature drops to between 145 and 165°F (63 and 74°C), about 30 minutes. Slice against the grain into thin strips and serve with white bread, dill pickles, and sliced onion.

SOUS VIDE CHUCK ROAST "RIBEYE"

Sous Vide Chuck Roast is incredibly flavorful, tender, and juicy. This 24-hour sous vide recipe transforms chuck roast into the most delicious beef roast that rivals an expensive prime rib.

Ingredients

2-4 lbs thick fatty, well marbled, chuck roast.

Kosher, Sea, or Pink Salt

1 TBSP Tallow

METHOD
Pan Seared

TOTAL TIME
Around 24.5 hours

SERVINGS
1-2

Instructions

- Vacuum seal a piece of salted chuck roast. If you do not have a vacuum sealer (or simply prefer convenience, place the chuck roast in a freezer zip lock back and use the water submersion method to "vacuum seal" the meat. Scan the QR code to see a demonstration.
- Set Sous Vide to the desired temperature, though most recommend a minimum of 130 degrees Fahrenheit for long cooks like those required for chuck steak.
- Place sealed chuck roast in water bath, and sous vide for approximately 24 hours. Make sure the meat is fully submerged. If using a zip lock, it may be beneficial to clip the top of the bag to your container. It may be helpful to put bowls or other objects in the water to hold the meat below the surface of the water.
- Remove chuck roast from the suis vide bath and bag and dry the surface of the steak thoroughly. Let it rest on the counter or in the fridge for approximately 15-20 minutes.
- Place 1 TBSP of tallow in ripping hot pan and sear the roast on all sided until a nice crust forms.
- Let rest for another 5 minutes, slice, salt to taste, and enjoy.
- **Optional:** dip every bite in delicious blue cheese butter or browned butter.

CHOPPED CHEESE

Our version of this NYC-bodega favorite (minus the roll) is a quick and easy-to-make Carnivore staple.

Ingredients

 1/2 lbs ground beef per serving

 1/4-1/2 cup cheese of your choosing

 2 TBSP Butter

 1/4 Cup Sour Cream

 Kosher, Sea, or Pink Salt

METHOD
Stove top

TOTAL TIME
30 Minutes

SERVINGS
1-2

Instructions

- Preheat a heavy bottom pan, place ground beef in pan, and shop up into as small of pieces as you desire with a spatula.
- Lightly dust the meat with salt, mix, and allow to cook until meat is a light pink color. Top with cheese, over and cook until cheese is melted. Chop/mix the cheesy ground beef and once fully mixed and cooked, put it in a bowl.
- Mix in 2 TBSP of butter until butter is melted then add 1/4 cup of sour cream.
- It doesn't look very appetizing, but damn, this is one heck of a delicious and affordable BEBBIS meal.

BLUE CHEESE BURGERS

The tang and creaminess of blue cheese make it a natural match for beefy burgers. Enjoy!

Ingredients

 Ground beef (12 oz)

 Blue Cheese (100 g)

 Butter (4 tbsp)

 Salt

METHOD

Stove top

TOTAL TIME

30 Minutes

SERVINGS

1-2

Instructions

- Shape 12 oz ground beef into (2) 6 oz patties
- Salt both sides of the burgers generously
- Heat a medium pan/cast iron skillet over medium high heat. After 1-2 minutes, add 2 tbsp butter to cover the base of the pan. Allow pan to continue heating.
- When butter starts to sizzle, add burgers.
- Flip burgers at half- way point (refer to cook times below.)
- Insert meat thermometer into the side of the burgers to check internal temperature (refer to temperature guide below.)
- Place burger's on a plate. Add 1 tbsp butter to each burger and bleu cheese. Cover plate in tin foil and allow to rest for 5 minutes.

CARNIVORE MEATBALLS

Super easy and fool proof. Keep some in your freezer for a quick meal or snack.

Ingredients

 2 lbs. Fatty ground beef

 1 Tbsp Salt

METHOD

Stove top

TOTAL TIME

40 Minutes

SERVINGS

1-2

Instructions

- Preheat the oven to 350°F (175°C).
- Combine ground meat and salt in a large bowl and mix thoroughly.
- Form into 2 to 3-ounce balls in the palm of your hand, approximately 12-16 meatballs.
- Arrange in a 9×13-inch (23×33-cm) glass baking dish and bake for 25-30 minutes until cooked. Balls should be packed snuggly. It's fine if the meatballs touch slightly while cooking.
- Remove from the oven and cool for 5 minutes. Serve warm.
- A typical serving size is 3 meatballs.
- Freeze the leftovers and reheat when you want to eat them again. Arrange the meatballs on a cookie sheet after baking and freeze. Then remove and store in a freezer-safe bag for up to 3 months. Reheat in the oven.

GROUND BEEF WITH TALLOW

A homemade comfort food that's moist and juicy on the inside and crispy on the outside

Ingredients

 16 oz 80/20 ground beef

 6 tbsp Tallow

 Salt

METHOD
Stove top

TOTAL TIME
15 Minutes

SERVINGS
1-2

Instructions

- Melt (6 tbsp) tallow over a medium high heat.
- Add ground beef and break into pieces with a wooden spoon/spatula.
- Add salt generously (you can't oversalt) while cooking.
- Serve hot.

BACON WRAPPED MEATLOAF

A homemade comfort food that's moist and juicy on the inside and crispy on the outside

Ingredients

 2 lb. ground beef

 1 lightly beaten egg

 ½ teaspoon salt

 1 lb. of bacon (room temperature is easier to wrap)

 8 oz. shredded cheddar or parmesan cheese (optional)

METHOD
Oven

TOTAL TIME
80-85 Minutes

SERVINGS
1-2

Instructions

- Preheat oven to 350°F. Prepare a large baking sheet with parchment paper
- In a large bowl, combine ground beef, breadcrumbs, egg, and salt. Mix until combined. Don't over mix. If using cheese, add now.
- Transfer meat to a baking sheet and form into a 10 x 5 loaf.
- Put the bacon slices over the sides and top, tucking the ends under the meatloaf. Make sure to tuck bacon in underneath the edges because the bacon will shrink during baking.
- Bake for 55-60 minutes or until until internal temperature on an instant read thermometer is 160°F.
- Remove the meatloaf from the oven and rest at room temperature for 10-15 minutes. Slice & serve.

Chapter Thirteen

CHICKEN RECIPES

FISH SAUCE CHICKEN WINGS

Tasty and addictive chicken wings with salty umami that will keep you reaching for more.

Ingredients

-  1 ½ lbs. Chicken wings
-  ¼ cup melted butter
-  1-2 Tbsp. Vietnamese Fish Sauce

METHOD

Stove top

TOTAL TIME

60 Minutes

SERVINGS

1-2

Instructions

- Preheat the oven to 425 degrees F (220 degrees C). Place chicken wings on a baking sheet.
- Cook chicken wings in the oven for 40-45 minutes until crispy and cooked through.
- Remove from oven and put wings in a bowl; pour chicken fat back over chicken wings
- Add ¼ cup of melted butter and 1-2 tbsp of fish sauce
- Enjoy!

PAN-SEARED CHICKEN THIGHS

With juicy meat and crispy golden brown skin, this thigh recipes is a crowd-pleasing dinner that comes together in under 30 minutes!

Ingredients

 4 – 6 bone-in, skin in chicken thights

 4 Tbsp butter, clarified butter, or ghee

 ½ tsp salt

METHOD
Stove Top

TOTAL TIME
30 minutes

SERVINGS
2-3

Instructions

- Preheat the oven to 400 degrees.
- Preheat a large oven-safe skillet over medium-high heat.
- Pat the chicken dry and season liberally with salt.
- Swirl 2 tablespoons of clarified butter in the pan to coat when hot.
- Place the chicken in the pan, skin side down. You should hear a nice sear happening. Allow to cook, without wiggling, flipping, or touching the chicken for 5 to 7 minutes to allow the skin to get nice and crispy. Adjust heat as needed to not burn.
- Flip the chicken, add the remaining clarified butter, and baste the chicken. Carefully transfer to the oven to finish cooking 8 to 10 minutes.
- Use an instant-read thermometer to check for a doneness temp of 165.
- Baste with butter and pan drippings and season with another sprinkle of salt before serving.

WHOLE SLOW ROASTED CHICKEN

Start with a pasture raised chicken for the best flavor. Provides a delicious weekend meal for the family or enough for several weekday meals.

Ingredients

 1 whole chicken (3-5 lbs) (pature-raised if possible for better flavor)

 3 tbs tallow or lard

 3 tsp sea salt

METHOD
Oven

TOTAL TIME
Around 4 hours

SERVINGS
3-4

Instructions

- Bring the chicken to room temperature
- Preheat the oven to 375°F (190°C)
- Clean the chicken and pat dry with a paper towel
- Rub tallow all over the chicken then rub it with the sea salt. You can use kitchen twine to tie the legs together if you like
- Place the chicken in a baking dish and roast for 30 minutes
- Reduce the temperature to 300°F (150°C). Add 2 tbs of water to the baking dish. Turn the chicken over. Cook for 3 more hours. Turn half-way.
- Transfer to a serving plate. Let cool for 10 minutes before serving. Best served hot in order to enjoy the delicious crunchy skin.

* To serve, use a pair of food scissors or a sharp knife to cut out the wing sections first. Next cut out the thighs and the drumsticks. For the torso, cut into halves along the spine then halves again. Drizzle pan juices over the chicken pieces and serve.

Chapter Fourteen

BACON/PORK RECIPES

PANCETTA STUFFED PORK CHOPS

Fancy but easy with lots of flavor and double the pork.

Ingredients

-  Pork Chop 6 oz (2)
-  Pancetta (2 oz)
-  Butter (4 tbsp)
-  Salt

METHOD
Oven

TOTAL TIME
60 minutes

SERVINGS
1-2

Instructions

- Preheat oven to 450 °F
- Brown diced pancetta over medium heat. When browned, remove pancetta from pan and remove pan from heat. Do not drain pan.
- Season pork chops generously in salt (you can't oversalt.) Cut a "pocket" along each side of the pork chops that you will later fill with the pancetta. Leave at least ¼ inch on each end and on the backside of the chop.
- Stuff each porkchop with 1 tbsp butter and pancetta.
- Add 2 tbsp of butter in pan w/ leftover pancetta. Add porkchops side by side.
- Place the skillet in the oven. Cook for 45 minutes.
- Drain excess fat into a tin container for later use.
- Return skillet and meat to oven for 10 additional minutes.
- Serve hot.

CRISPY PORK BELLY

Pork belly is salty, rich, meaty, and melts in your mouth.

Ingredients

 3 lb. Pork Belly with skin

 3 Tbsp avocado oil

 1 Tbsp sea salt

METHOD

Oven

TOTAL TIME

Around 2 hours

SERVINGS

1-2

Instructions

- Preheat oven to 350 degrees F.
- Using a knife, score the skin of the pork belly.
- Use a basting brush to brush the olive oil or avocado oil on both sides of the pork belly. Sprinkle generously with salt.
- Place the pork belly into a baking dish skin side up, and bake for 1 hour.
- Increase oven to 425 degrees F and bake for an additional 45 minutes.
- Change oven to broil and broil the pork belly on high for 5 minutes to crisp up.
- Allow the pork belly to rest for 10 minutes before cutting into 1-inch slices.

PARMESAN PORK MEATBALLS

Delicious as finger food or topped with a cheesy cream sauce.

Ingredients

 2 pounds ground pork (use Heritage pork for more flavor)

 1 cup shredded parmesan cheese

 2 eggs optional

 1 teaspoon sea salt

METHOD

Oven

TOTAL TIME

50 minutes

SERVINGS

1-2

Instructions

- Mix together the ground pork, parmesan cheese, and optional eggs. The cheese has plenty of salt, but you may want to cook a bit of the meat mixture in a pan on the stove and adjust the salt if needed - add 1 teaspoon of sea salt at a time until you get the saltiness that you like.
- Preheat broiler to high. Raise rack to the second slot down from the top in the oven. Line a metal baking tray with shallow sides with parchment paper.
- While the oven pre-heats, roll meatballs into desired size and place on the lined baking sheet; touching but not overlapping. Make sure your meatballs are all uniform size so they cook evenly.
- Once preheated, broil the meatballs for 5 minutes, or until tops start to darken. If you are freezing the meatballs, remove them now and cool, then transfer to a freezer bag. Reheat/finish cooking from thawed, 350F for 20 minutes or until cooked through.
- Move meatballs to the middle of the oven and turn the oven to 'bake' and 350* and bake for an additional 15-20 minutes, depending on how big your meatballs are.
- To check doneness, cut meatball in half. Slight pink in the middle is okay, as they will continue cooking as they cool.
- Serve your meatballs, topping with more cheese or cream sauce as desired.

Chapter Fifteen

SEAFOOD/ FISH RECIPES

SALMON ROASTED WITH BUTTER OR GHEE

Simple and tasty. Perfectly cooked salmon separates into big, soft flakes and is bright pink in the center. It will continue to cook a little more out of the oven.

Ingredients

 8 oz Salmon filet

 4 tbsp Tallow

 4 tbsp Butter or Ghee

 Salt

METHOD
Stove Top

TOTAL TIME
30 minutes

SERVINGS
1-2

Instructions

- Melt 4 oz butter or Ghee over medium high heat
- Season salmon on both sides with salt
- Place 12 oz salmon in pan skin side down
- Cook skin side down 6-9 minutes
- Flip salmon cook addition 1-2 minutes
- Pour remaining tallow onto salmon
- Add 2 tbsp butter and allow salmon to rest for 3 minutes
- Serve 8 oz salmon, save 4 oz salmon for tomorrows first meal.

BACON WRAPPED SHRIMP

Wrapping things in bacon makes everything better! A great snack or appetizer and easy to make.

Ingredients

 16 large shrimp, peeled & deveined

 8 strips of thin cut bacon or prosciutto sliced in half long-ways (partially cook thick cuts of bacon for additional time before wrapping if needed; par-cooked bacon is required for a crispy bacon texture if preferred)

 ¼ tsp sea salt

 2 Tbsp melted butter

METHOD

Oven

TOTAL TIME

30 minutes

SERVINGS

1-2

Instructions

- Preheat oven to 425 degrees F. Line a sheet pan with aluminum foil for easy clean up.
- Place shrimp in a medium bowl. Add melted butter and salt. Stir.
- Using a sharp knife, cut the bacon strips lengthwise. Arrange bacon slices, leaving space around each, on oven safe rack placed inside a baking sheet. Bake 5 to 10 minutes depending on the thickness of your bacon. It should still be pliable when you remove it from the oven.
- When partially cooked bacon slices are cool enough to handle (about 5 minutes after you remove from oven), wrap each slice of bacon around one raw shrimp, securing with a toothpick; return to oven safe rack. Repeat with remaining shrimp.
- Bake 10 minutes more until shrimp are pink and bacon is cooked through. Serve.

SALMON WITH CREAM CHEESE SAUCE

With its rich and tangy flavor, this sauce is the perfect addition to any seafood but is particularly delicious with salmon.

Ingredients

-  4 – 6 oz. salmon fillets
-  2 Tbsp butter (for sauteing fish)
-  ½ cup of chicken stock or bone broth
-  4 oz. cream cheese
-  ½ tsp salt

METHOD	TOTAL TIME	SERVINGS
Stove Top	30 minutes	1-2

Instructions

- Cook salmon fillets in oven, cast iron pan, or grill until cooked through. Prepare sauce while salmon is cooking.
- Combine stock, cream cheese, and salt in a small sauce pan and whisk over medium heat until combined and creamy. Spoon over salmon fillets.

PRAWNS WITH BUTTER & BACON

Three fantastic flavors combine for a tasty and easy-to-make entrée.

Ingredients

-  2 tbs unsalted butter
-  8 slices of bacon, excess fat trimmed
-  12 oz shrimp, deveined, and peeled-tail on or off as preferred
-  Sea salt to taste

METHOD
Stove Top

TOTAL TIME
15-20 minutes

SERVINGS
1-2

Instructions

- Melt the butter in a skillet.
- Cut the bacon into 1" pieces and sauté until starting to turn crispy.
- Add the shrimp and cook on each side for 3-4 minutes or until cooked through.
- Serve, garnished with a sprinkle of sea salt.

SURF & TURF – RIBEYE STEAK & SHRIMP

Tender steak and plump shrimp are quickly cooked to perfection.

Ingredients

 Ribeye 8 oz

 Shrimp (6)

 Butter (6 tbsp)

 Salt

METHOD
Stove Top

TOTAL TIME
30 minutes

SERVINGS
1-2

Instructions

- Season steak generously in salt.
- Cook 12 oz ribeye on grill, in pan, or in oven to desired temperature. (refer to "Best Way to Cook Ribeye Guide".)
- If cooking in pan or oven, cook in 2 tbsp butter and add additional 2 tbsp butter afterwards.
- If cooking on grill, add 4 tbsp after grilling.
- Save 4 oz of ribeye (1/3) for tomorrow's first meal.
- If using raw shrimp, heat pan over medium high heat.
- Add 2 tbsp butter after 1 minute.

Chapter Sixteen

EGG RECIPES

STEAK & BUTTER GAL'S STEAMED EGG PUDDING

Perfectly smooth, silky, and glossy every single time.

Ingredients

 2 Pasture-Raised Eggs

 Lukewarm Water (or Bone Broth for gourmet version)

METHOD
Stove Top

TOTAL TIME
6-10 minutes

SERVINGS
1-2

Instructions

- Set saute pan with water on stove on high heat until water is at a rolling boiling.
- Mix/whisk eggs then add and mix in your choice of liquid in 1:1 ratio.
- Carefully place bowl with egg mixture into water bath and cover with lid to steam. Crack lid slightly so some steam can escape. Turn heat down to medium. Too high heat will create air bubbles.
- Steam for 3-4 minutes on medium but keep an eye on it to ensure it's cooking properly. The water should be at a rolling boil at all times for proper steaming. It's done cooking when middle is completely set and not liquid at all. It will be jello-like.
- Drizzle with butter and enjoy.

Steak and Butter Gal's Youtube Channel

DEVILED EGGS

Great as a quick meal, snack, or side dish.

Ingredients

 12 eggs

 8 strips of bacon

 4 good size chicken livers

 1T Redmond's Real Salt or Maldon Sea Salt

 2 tablespoons of water

METHOD

Stove Top

TOTAL TIME

30 minutes

SERVINGS

1-2

Instructions

- Place eggs in a saucepan and cover with cold water. Bring water to a boil and immediately remove the pan from the heat. Cover and let eggs cook in hot water for 11 minutes. Remove eggs from hot water and rinse with very cold water.
- While eggs are cooking, fry the bacon extra crispy then set aside your skillet with the bacon drippings. Pat down bacon and set aside.
- In the remaining bacon drippings, fry up the chicken livers until thoroughly cooked. Place into blender.
- Crack, roll, and peel your eggs and cut in half. Scoop out the hard-boiled yolks and place into the blender. Add salt and 2 tablespoons of water. Blend until smooth.
- Crumble the crispy bacon into small but not fine pieces.
- Spread out the empty halved egg whites. Inside each half, place a small pinch of minced bacon. Using a spoon, cover bacon with the blended liver and egg yolk mousse. Refrigerate until serving.

SIMPLE GROUND BEEF & EGGS

A protein-packed breakfast scramble. Cook eggs any way you like and combine with ground beef.

Ingredients

-  Leftover simple ground beef (4 oz)
-  Eggs (2)
-  Butter (2 tbsp)
-  Salt

METHOD
Stove Top

TOTAL TIME
20 minutes

SERVINGS
1-2

Instructions

- **Option 1:** Heat 2 tbsp butter in pan, add leftover ground beef, scramble eggs in beef fat and butter, salt generously (you can't oversalt.)
- **Option 2:** Use hard boiled eggs (or eggs any way) and eat w/ ground beef. – add 2tbsp butter to beef, salt generously (you can't oversalt.)

PANCETTA & EGGS

Salty pancetta is the perfect complement to scrambled eggs. Top with a little parmesan if desired for another layer of flavor.

Ingredients

 Pancetta (2oz)

 Eggs (2)

 Butter (2 tbsp)

 Salt

METHOD
Stove Top

TOTAL TIME
10-15 minutes

SERVINGS
1-2

Instructions

- Heat a pan over medium heat
- After 1 minute heating add 1 tbsp butter
- As butter sizzles, add pancetta
- Cook pancetta 3-4 minutes. Add 2 eggs and 1 tbsp butter to pan.
- Scramble eggs and pancetta until desired doneness.

BREAKFAST SAUSAGE, EGG, & CHEESE SCRAMBLE

A hearty meal for breakfast or any time of day.

Ingredients

 10-12 pork breakfast sausages removed from their casings

 7 eggs

 8-10 oz. cup shredded cheese

½ cup Heavy Cream

 Sea Salt to taste

METHOD
Stove Top

TOTAL TIME
20 minutes

SERVINGS
1-2

Instructions

- Place sausage in a large skillet. Cook over medium high heat until sausage is evenly browned, breaking up sausage with a spatula or spoon as needed.
- While sausage is cooking, beat eggs and heavy cream together in a mixing bowl.
- Remove cooked sausage to a separate bowl. Pour eggs into the skillet. Add cheese and cook just until eggs are set.
- Stir in sausage, add salt to taste, and serve warm.

BAKED SCOTCH EGGS

Protein-packed and delicious, these are the perfect breakfast, lunch or dinner.

Ingredients

2 pounds of ground beef

2 tsp salt

10 large hard-boiled eggs

METHOD

Stove Top

TOTAL TIME

35 minutes

SERVINGS

1-2

Instructions

- Preheat oven to 350 F.
- Line a large baking tray with a baking sheet.
- Place the ground beef into a large mixing bowl and season with salt. Hand mix the ground beef and shape it into ten equally-sized meatballs. Place the meatballs on the baking pan and flatten them.
- Then place one boiled egg in the center of each beef circle and wrap the meat around the egg, ensuring no gaps or holes.
- Bake for 10-15 minutes, then flip to cook the other side. If you like a crispier finish, turn the broiler on for the last few minutes to finish them off.

CLOUD EGGS

Just as fluffy as they are delicate and delicious. An Instagram sensation that's worth trying in your own kitchen.

Ingredients

- 4 eggs
- Pinch of fine sea salt
- 1/4 cup Parmesan (grated)
- Garnish: crumbled bacon or pancetta

METHOD
Stove Top

TOTAL TIME
20 minutes

SERVINGS
1-2

Instructions

- Preheat the oven to 400 F and arrange a baking rack in the top third of the oven. Line a baking sheet with parchment paper, a silpat, or lightly grease it.
- Separate the eggs, putting the yolks in a small bowl and the whites in a big bowl. A copper bowl works best for beating egg whites, but any bowl will suffice. Set the yolks aside.
- Whisk the egg whites until they're frothy—use the biggest whisk you have to beat as much air as possible into them or a hand mixer.
- Add a pinch of salt and keep whisking until firm peaks form—when you lift the whisk out of the whites the peak that forms should hold its shape.
- Gently fold in the cheese. Scrape the side of the bowl with a rubber or silicone spatula, then under the egg white mixture and back up the other side of the bowl, lifting and turning the egg whites and the cheese together without causing the egg whites to lose too much air.
- Spoon the egg whites into 4 equal mounds on the baking sheet. Use the back of a spoon to make egg yolk-size wells in the center of each one.
- Bake the clouds until they just start to color - about 5 minutes.
- Gently spoon a yolk into the center well of each cloud.
- Return to the oven and bake until the yolk is runny, 3 minutes, or up to fully set, 8 minutes.
- Garnish eggs with a pinch of salt or some crumbled bacon or pancetta and serve. Eggs are best served right from the oven and do not store well.

Chapter Seventeen

TREAT RECIPES

DUCK FAT FRENCH FRIES

Savory duck fat adds a wonderful delicate flavor to the fries. One of Dr. Kiltz's favorite but occasional treats.

Ingredients

 4 large Russet potatoes, peeled and cut into ¼-1/2 inch strips

 2 cups Duck fat (Beef tallow or lard can be used as well)

 Redmond's Real Salt or Maldon Sea Salt (to taste)

METHOD
Stove Top

TOTAL TIME
35 minutes plus soaking time

SERVINGS
1-2

Instructions

- Cut French fries and soak in cold water for at least 1 hour, better 8 hours, ideally 24 hours
- Fill large pot with duck fat, tallow, or lard (less than 50% full to avoid hot oil from spilling over during frying) and heat to 325 degrees
- Remove potatoes from the water and pat dry to remove excess water.
- Add potatoes to hot oil with at least 1-inch of oil above the potatoes and par cook until potatoes are tannish/very light brown, usually around 5 to 10 minutes.
- Remove potatoes and place on cooling rack or into a paper bag to remove excess oil and let drain on rack. Repeat until all of the potatoes are par cooked.
- Heat oil to 350 degrees
- Add potatoes back to oil in similar size batches and cook for 2-5 minutes until golden brown
- Put fries back on cooling rack or paper bag and season with salt

KILTZ'S FULL-FAT ICE CREAM

Full fat, but guilt-free. Enjoy as a treat or even a full meal (on occasion). With or without sugar, this is a delicious and rich ice cream with all of the healthy fat your body needs.

Ingredients

 1 Pint of Heavy Cream (ideally locally sourced and grass-fed)

 1 whole egg (or 5 egg yolks)

 1 vanilla bean pod (or 1 tbsp vanilla bean paste/vanilla extract)

 1-2 tbsp of sugar (optional not required) or honey/maple syrup/ or alternative sweetener

 1-3 pinches of salt- optional and to taste

METHOD
Stove Top

TOTAL TIME
60 minutes

SERVINGS
1-2

Instructions

- Shake cream and pour into a large bowl.
- Add sugar and egg.
- Split vanilla bean(s) lengthwise and scrape the tiny seeds from inside the bean using the edge of a knife. For maximum flavor, steep the bean and seeds in the cream mixture for about 10 minutes. Remove the bean pod(s).
- Whisk until well combined and frothy.
- Pour into an ice cream machine and follow the manufacturer's instructions.

"BEBBIS is all about simplicity. By streamlining your food choices, simplifying meal prep, and eating less frequently, you're providing your body with its best fuel and giving your mind and body extra time to rest, restore, and be inspired."

Made in United States
North Haven, CT
18 August 2024

56246309R00077